Temple

of Invention

Smithsonian American Art Museum
National Portrait Gallery
in association with Scala Publishers Ltd

Charles J. Robertson

Temple
of Invention

History of a National Landmark

Temple of Invention:
History of a National Landmark

By Charles J. Robertson

Chief, Publications: Theresa J. Slowik
Designers: Robert Killian, Karen Siatras
Editor: Susan L. Efird

Published in conjunction with the exhibition of the same name,
on view at the historic Patent Office Building, Washington, D.C.,
July 2006–July 2007. Organized by the National Portrait Gallery
and the Smithsonian American Art Museum.

Published in 2006 by
Scala Publishers Ltd
Northburgh House
10 Northburgh Street
London EC1V 0AT

Cover: Patent Office Building, 1846. Daguerreotype by John
Plumbe Jr. Library of Congress, see p. 28

Border and page 112: Central encaustic tile panel, Great Hall,
south wing. From original drawing by Cluss & Schulze, 1884

Title page: Patent examiners at work, 1869. Detail of hand-
colored illustration from *Harper's Weekly,* July 10, 1869. National
Portrait Gallery

Back cover: Robert Mills's curving staircase, 1997. National
Portrait Gallery

Printed in Singapore
10 9 8 7 6 5 4 3 2 1

Library of Congress Cataloging-in-Publication Data

Robertson, Charles (Charles J.)
    Temple of invention : history of a national landmark / by
Charles J. Robertson.
       p.   cm.
Includes bibliographical references and index.

ISBN 1-85759-385-5 (softcover)
1. Smithsonian American Art Museum. 2. National Portrait
Gallery (Smithsonian Institution) 3. United States. Patent and
Trademark Office—Buildings—History. 4. Public buildings—
Remodeling for other use—Washington (D.C.) 5. Art museum
architecture—Conservation and restoration—Washington (D.C.)
6. Washington (D.C.)—Buildings, structures, etc. I. Title.

N857.R63 2006
725'.1—dc22
                                              2005023813

Contents

Temple of Invention:
History of a National Landmark
and the accompanying exhibition are
made possible by generous support from
Allan J. and Reda R. Riley

Additional support for the publication was
provided by Furthermore, a program of the
J. M. Kaplan Fund

Foreword

In July 2006 the National Portrait Gallery and the Smithsonian American Art Museum reopened after more than six years of renovation of the Patent Office Building. The occasion seems the perfect opportunity to offer a popular history of this venerable building that not only surveys its construction but also brings to life the colorful figures and events that it has witnessed over almost two centuries. This book is the first published history of the building, which has been a National Historic Landmark since 1965.

The Patent Office Building has been a focus of interest to Charles Robertson during his twenty-four years of service at the Smithsonian American Art Museum, including sixteen as deputy director. The coincidence of his retirement and the need for this history made him the logical choice as author. Any study of the building, however, must begin with Douglas Evelyn's exhaustive dissertation *A Public Building for a New Democracy: The Patent Office Building in the Nineteenth Century*. Commencing with his position as deputy director of the Portrait Gallery from 1969 to 1979, he has devoted a substantial part of his life to the study of and publication about this noble edifice.

This book and its accompanying exhibition of the same title are a collaboration between the American Art Museum and the Portrait Gallery. Together the exhibition and book will bring new information, insight, and appreciation to the building's rich and varied history.

Elizabeth Broun
The Margaret and Terry Stent Director
Smithsonian American Art Museum

Marc Pachter
Director, National Portrait Gallery
Smithsonian Institution

Beginnings

Walt Whitman called it "that noblest of Washington buildings." A masterpiece of Greek Revival design, the Patent Office Building was constructed wing by wing between 1836 and 1868, covering two city blocks when completed. It was conceived as a "temple of invention," an expression of America's creative genius and technical superiority. Its enormous galleries once displayed thousands of models of patented inventions from the cotton gin to the first telephone. Home to the Patent Office for almost a hundred years, the building was saved from demolition and transferred to the Smithsonian Institution in 1958 to house two museums and their art collections. It once again fulfills its purpose in celebrating America's creative achievements.

The importance of patents was recognized in the earliest days of the fledgling Republic. Article I of the U.S. Constitution gave Congress the authority "to promote the progress of science and useful arts by securing for limited times to authors and inventors the exclusive right to their respective writings and inventions." This clause was approved without debate by the Constitutional Convention in 1788, but it was not until two years later that Congress passed the first statute to implement patent procedures for the new country.

The law required an application—accompanied by a description, drawing, and model—to be filed with the secretary of state, then Thomas Jefferson. The secretary

Blodgett's Hotel, 1803 (detail; see fig. 3, p. 12). This building (at right) was the home of the Patent Office for twenty-six years until it burned in 1836. The White House is faintly visible in the distance (at far left).

of state, the secretary of war, and the attorney general then each reviewed the application to determine "whether the invention or discovery [was] sufficiently useful and important to merit a patent." When issued, the patent was signed personally by the three secretaries and by the president himself (George Washington), after which it was impressed with the Great Seal of the United States. Only three patents were issued the first year. Needless to say, these distinguished officials had more pressing demands on their time than patent applications, and delays were inevitable.

To remedy the situation, Congress in 1793 passed an act that went almost to the opposite extreme in revising the procedure. The secretary of state was required to issue a patent regardless of originality, usefulness, or existence of a patent for the same invention. Disputes would be resolved in the courts, not by the Patent Office. Granted for fourteen years, a patent required a filing fee of thirty dollars, a substantial sum at the time, which was deposited in a separate account with the Treasury Department to support the costs of patent operations. Thus the Patent Office until 1865 enjoyed a unique status as the only self-supporting bureau of the federal government. The 1793 legislation, which remained in effect for forty-three years, speeded up the flow of patents, but also precipitated serious new problems, to be discussed later.

The most important patent under the new system was granted to Eli Whitney in 1794 for the cotton gin (fig. 1). Whitney was forced to undertake a lengthy series of court battles to defend his patent and ultimately collected some $90,000 in royalties, then an enormous amount. Other notable patents were granted to Eleuthère du Pont in 1804 for the improved manufacture of gunpowder and in 1809 to Robert Fulton for the steamboat.

Fig. 1
Eli Whitney's cotton gin, courtroom model, ca. 1800. This early invention brought prosperity to both planters in the South and textile mills in the North.

In 1800 the State Department, along with the rest of the federal government, moved from Philadelphia to the new capital of Washington, D.C. The department at that time had only eight employees. Because of the influx of patent applications, Secretary of State James Madison in 1802 hired William Thornton as his clerk to handle patent matters, at an annual salary of $1,400 (fig. 2). Thornton was a man of many talents. Born in 1761 in Tortola in the British West Indies, he was raised in England and trained as a physician in Scotland. He immigrated to the United States in 1787 and six years later, without any architectural training, won the competition for the design of the U.S. Capitol. Thornton also designed a number of distinguished private residences, including two for granddaughters of Martha Washington. By appointment of George Washington, he served as a commissioner of the District of Columbia from 1794 to 1802.

Thornton was the State Department's only patent clerk until 1810, when an assistant was finally authorized. Although not required to do so by law, Thornton nevertheless undertook a patent search for each new application. If the proposed invention had already been patented or was not sufficiently novel, he would notify the applicant and offer to refund the filing fee if the application were withdrawn. By law, however, the applicant could decline the offer and insist that a patent be issued.

To alleviate overcrowded conditions in temporary buildings, the government in 1810 purchased Blodgett's Hotel, the largest private structure in Washington

Fig. 2
William Thornton, 1804. A man of broad interests, he headed the Patent Office for twenty-six years until his death in 1828.

(fig. 3). Almost two decades earlier, promoter Samuel Blodgett had retained James Hoban, architect of the White House, to construct the three-story brick building as first prize in a lottery. The lottery failed, and Blodgett went bankrupt. After remaining vacant for many years, the structure was renovated by the government, and the Patent Office and the much larger Post Office Department moved in as joint tenants.

During the War of 1812, the British occupied Washington in 1814 and burned the White House and the Capitol. With instructions to destroy all

Fig. 3
Blodgett's Hotel (at right), 1803. This view from Pennsylvania Avenue illustrates how rural Washington was after the government moved there in 1800.

government buildings, troops advanced on Blodgett's Hotel. William Thornton met them there and, by his account, persuaded them that the patent models were useful to all mankind and that destroying them would be the equivalent of the burning of the great library at Alexandria in ancient times. Blodgett's Hotel was spared and, in fact, was used temporarily for the 1814–15 session of Congress. Thornton remained superintendent of patents until his death in 1828.

Thornton's successor discontinued the practice of a patent search and a notice to applicants of potential problems, and, as a result, the courts became overburdened with lawsuits involving patent disputes. Nothing prevented an applicant from copying a patent's specifications, drawings, and model and securing his own patent for the same invention. Often these patent grants, bearing the signature of the president and the Great Seal of the United States, were presented to unsuspecting investors in the fraudulent sales of licensing rights. Such sales were estimated to total as much as $500,000 per year. The system was described as "onerous to the courts, ruinous to the parties and injurious to society."

Over the years the number of patent filings increased exponentially (fig. 4). In 1830 Blodgett's Hotel was enlarged, and the Patent Office moved into the addition, but that space soon proved inadequate. With the hiring of additional clerks and an accumulation of more than 7,000 models crammed into every available space, the Patent Office desperately needed a building of its own, as well as a reform of the patent law.

Patents Issued during Each Decade

1790–99	268
1800–09	911
1810–19	1,998
1820–29	2,697
1830–39	5,641
1840–49	5,902
1850–59	21,302
1860–69	77,355
1870–79	137,741
1880–89	205,476
1890–99	234,749
1900–09	314,478
1910–19	397,543
1920–29	443,942
1930–39	485,205

Fig. 4
Number of patents issued. After a slow start, the rate of patents increased rapidly over the years.

The Turning Point

The nation's capital in 1836 was a town of some 20,000 souls and dirt streets that turned to mud in rain. Hogs ran wild, but could be seized and sold at auction if caught south of Massachusetts Avenue. Congress was in session for only three months in some years, and congressmen stayed in boarding houses during their sojourn. After a visit in 1842, novelist Charles Dickens wrote about his impression of the city: "It is sometimes called the City of Magnificent Distances, but it might with greater propriety be termed the City of Magnificent Intentions. . . . Spacious avenues, that begin in nothing, and lead nowhere; streets, mile-long, that only want houses, roads and inhabitants; public buildings that need but a public to be complete" (fig. 5).

However, Frances Trollope, another English visitor, writing in 1832, was more charitable in assessing the new capital: "I was delighted with the whole aspect of Washington. . . . It has been laughed at by foreigners, and even by natives, because the original plan of the city was upon an enormous scale, and but a very small part of it has been as yet executed. But I confess I see nothing in the least degree ridiculous about it; the original design, which was as beautiful as it was extensive, had been in no way departed from, and all that has been done has been done well." The country was in an entrepreneurial mood. Canal systems and railroads were being built, and westward expansion was under way.

Fig. 5
City of Washington from Beyond the Navy Yard, 1833 (detail; see p. 16). The Navy Yard is at center on the river. The Capitol (above) and the White House (far left) are exaggerated in scale.

Fig. 5
City of Washington from Beyond the Navy Yard, 1833. The still sparsely settled city was best viewed from across the Anacostia River.

Fig. 6
John Ruggles, 1834. A senator from Maine, he was largely responsible for the new Patent Office Building and a revised patent law.

The year 1836 marked a turning point in the history of the Patent Office. Congress enacted a radically new patent law, construction began on a grand new building for the office, and Blodgett's Hotel burned, destroying all of the patent records and models within it. Two men were largely responsible for inaugurating the new era.

John Ruggles was elected a new senator from Maine in 1835 (fig. 6). He had been speaker of the Maine House of Representatives and a justice of the Maine Supreme Court. An amateur inventor himself, he began an investigation of the sad state of affairs at the Patent Office immediately after his arrival in Washington. That same year Henry Ellsworth was appointed superintendent of the Patent Office (fig. 7). Son of a U.S. Supreme Court justice, Ellsworth had been president of the Aetna Insurance Company, chief commissioner of Indian tribes, and mayor of Hartford, Connecticut. After reorganizing the Patent Office and eliminating a crushing backlog, Ellsworth submitted a lengthy report through the secretary of state to Senator Ruggles that recommended revising the patent law and constructing new quarters for the office. Largely through Ruggles's efforts, Congress passed legislation to overhaul the patent system and appropriated $108,000 to erect a Patent Office building.

Fig. 7
Henry L. Ellsworth, ca. 1850. He was the influential superintendent of the Patent Office from 1835 to 1845.

President Andrew Jackson signed the act into law on July 4, 1836 (fig. 8). It established a new position of examiner of patents to conduct a patent search in both the United States and Europe, using an extensive new patent library. Patents would be granted for utility, originality, and patentability under a new numbering system. The requirement for models would remain a unique feature of the American system. A separately appointed board of arbitrators would hear any appeals from the examiner's decision. Ellsworth was appointed the first commissioner of patents. In honor of his dedicated work, Senator Ruggles was awarded U.S. Patent Number One for a steam engine to be used on inclined planes.

The new law became a model for the world and gave the United States a tremendous boost in its industrial independence from Europe. As Abraham Lincoln later noted, "The patent system added the fuel of interest to the fire of genius." Already twice as many patents had been issued in the United States as in either England or France. The 1836 act has remained the backbone of U.S. patent law ever since.

In addition, Congress set certain requirements for the new Patent Office Building. In 1833 fire had gutted the Treasury Building and two years later destroyed fifty-two acres of New York City. The new structure clearly must be fireproof. Furthermore, it should be large enough to meet the needs of the Patent Office for the next fifty years, a remarkably ambitious vision for a young nation with modest resources. Suitable galleries should provide for the display of patent models and "be kept open . . . for public inspection," thereby establishing the Patent Office as an important destination for public visitation and display. Another requirement was that the building be constructed of the same sandstone from the government-owned quarry at Aquia Creek, Virginia, as had been used for the

Fig. 8
Andrew Jackson, 1836–37. The president is depicted standing on the south portico of the White House with the Capitol in the background. He selected the site, plan, and architect for the Patent Office Building.

Capitol and the White House. Funding for the new edifice would come from the surplus in patent filing fees that had accumulated in the Treasury.

Architecture was not widely recognized as a profession in those early days. There were gentlemen architects such as Thomas Jefferson and William Thornton, and there were practicing architects who learned their skills through apprenticeship and experience. Intimately familiar with construction methods and materials, they supervised the erection of the buildings they designed. These architects were often expected to act as general contractors, procuring building materials and laborers, negotiating contracts, and making payments as construction progressed.

One aspiring young architect was William Parker Elliot, who was born in Washington in 1807 and had studied in the office of prominent Washington architect George Hadfield. Elliot's father had been chief patent clerk from 1816 to 1829. Through his father's influence, Elliot was granted permission in 1829 to set up a freelance drafting table in the Patent Office where he made patent drawings.

Despite his connections, however, he was never hired by the Patent Office. After a heated dispute with the patent superintendent, Elliot was removed from the building in 1834 by order of President Jackson. With much bitterness, he then opened an office of his own and looked for opportunities elsewhere. The prominent architectural partnership of Ithiel Town and Alexander Jackson Davis in New York City, interested in expanding its practice, retained him as its agent to seek commissions in the nation's capital.

By 1834 efforts were afoot in Congress to authorize a new building for the Patent Office. At Elliot's request, Davis prepared plans for it (fig. 9), designing a monumental Greek Revival structure with a giant Doric portico modeled after the Parthenon in Athens (fig. 10). Elliot borrowed architectural motifs from Davis's plan and adapted them to a rectangular structure around an open court, with similar Parthenon-like porticoes on the south and north sides of the building. The entrepreneurial twenty-nine-year-old Elliot then took his drawings to Ruggles's Senate committee, which recommended them for adoption by President Jackson. There is no record that Elliot ever had an architectural practice or that he ever supervised the construction of a building. His only qualifications were that he had studied with Hadfield and had traveled abroad to view architectural monuments there.

Fig. 9
Second project for a patent building, 1834 (detail; all rights reserved, the Metropolitan Museum of Art). This drawing by Alexander J. Davis was probably adapted by William P. Elliot for his plan of the Patent Office Building.

Fig. 10
The Parthenon. The portico of the Patent Office Building was modeled after the Parthenon. This lithograph, composed by Alexander J. Davis in 1834, depicts an idealized version of the building.

Robert Mills in Charge

If there is a hero and a martyr of the Patent Office Building, it is Robert Mills (fig. 11). Born in Charleston, South Carolina, in 1781, Mills received an academic education at Charleston College. He caught the eye of Thomas Jefferson, who invited him to advance his architectural education by using the extensive library at Monticello. Armed with letters of introduction from Jefferson, Mills spent two years traveling around the country to study buildings he considered architecturally significant. For the next five years, he apprenticed in Philadelphia with the eminent British-born architect Benjamin Henry Latrobe. During a distinguished career over the following twenty-five years, Mills designed and constructed a large number of buildings as diverse as churches, private residences, courthouses, jails, hospitals, and monuments. Most of his commissions were in the South, but some were in Philadelphia and Baltimore. He summarized his approach to classical architecture in these words: "I have always deprecated the servile copying of the buildings of antiquity; we have the same principles and materials to work upon that the ancients had, and we should adapt these materials to the habits and customs of our people as they did to theirs." Mills specialized in fireproof construction through the use of masonry vaults, and his County Records Office in Charleston (1822–27) was known colloquially as "The Fireproof Building." He promoted himself as America's first native-born, professionally trained architect.

Fig. 11
Robert Mills and his wife, ca. 1851.
Mills was the supervising architect of the
Patent Office Building from 1836 to 1851.

When his engagement with South Carolina's Board of Public Works expired, Mills looked for new opportunities, and in 1830 he moved his wife and five children to the nation's capital. He was soon employed in the Land Office, and was hired as a clerk in the Patent Office immediately following William Elliot's dismissal. During this period, Mills was permitted to undertake outside commissions, designing four customhouses in New England for the government. After President Andrew Jackson's home, the Hermitage, near Nashville, was damaged by fire in 1834, the president asked for Mills's advice in reconstructing it. Although Mills was careful to maintain political neutrality, most of his appointments were in fact secured through Jacksonian democrats.

In competition with Elliot, Mills had also submitted a plan for the new Patent Office Building. Mills and Elliot each lobbied members of Congress to endorse his respective plan. In the final legislation, Congress left to President Jackson the decision of which plan to adopt. On July 6, 1836, only two days after signing the authorizing legislation, Jackson appointed "Robert Mills as Architect to aid in forming the plans, making proper changes therein from time to time, and seeing to the erection of said . . . [Patent Office Building] in substantial conformity to the plans hereby adopted, which are, in their general outlines, that annexed by Mr. Elliot." So the general outline of Elliot's plan was approved, but Mills would be responsible for executing it, with some latitude to make changes.

At the same time, President Jackson designated as the site for the new building a prominent square between the Capitol and the White House (fig. 12). Major Pierre L'Enfant in his 1791 plan for the city had reserved this space for a nondenominational church or pantheon to honor the nation's heroes. The Patent Office Building, described as "a temple of the useful arts," was deemed a worthy substitute for the

Fig. 12
City of Washington, 1836 (detail). The site chosen for the Patent Office Building between the Capitol and White House is outlined in red. Colored backgrounds indicate various wards. Shaded blocks show areas with buildings.

practical young Republic. In a concurrent decision, Jackson rejected Elliot's plan for a new Treasury building and approved Mills's plan, also charging Mills with oversight of that building's construction. Mills's salary was set at $1,800 per year plus $500 for drawings. He adopted for himself the title "Architect of Public Buildings."

President Jackson privately informed Elliot that he had appointed Mills architect in charge of construction of the Patent Office because Mills "had come well-recommended as an experienced builder of fire-proof buildings" and because Elliot was "too young and inexperienced." Elliot confessed his disappointment in his diary, but he could hardly have been surprised at the president's decision. He was

eventually paid $300 for his plans. Thus began a vendetta by Elliot against Mills that would last for fifteen years. During this period, Elliot launched attacks against Mills at every opportunity by lobbying influential politicians, contacting newspapers and journals, and writing letters to government officials. Mills noted that Elliot "resorted to every means to injure my professional standing."

Construction began immediately on the new building and so did the problems. Elliot's approved plans have unfortunately been lost, but apparently they consisted only of an "outline" plan of the interior and elevations of the exterior. Thus Mills was left with designing most of the interior himself. Congress's $108,000 appropriation covered only the south wing of the plan's grand rectangular edifice. Another problem was that the figure was based on Elliot's estimate for a brick structure with wooden floors and ceilings that, in Mills's opinion, did not meet the fireproof requirement of the legislation. Mills proceeded to have the foundations laid in granite and hoped that granite or marble could be used for the rest of the building. However, Martin Van Buren, who had been elected president by that time, insisted on the less expensive Aquia Creek sandstone.

Mills designed three stories with spacious interiors and gallery spaces for the display of patent models, agricultural implements, and other objects of interest. His system of fireproof groined masonry vaults, supported by piers and columns, which had worked so well in his previous public buildings, allowed maximum natural light and flexibility for display cases and other uses. In a deviation from Elliot's plan, Mills designed a splendid double-curving staircase in a projecting apse at the rear of the entrance lobby (see illustration on back cover). By this placement of the stair, he achieved open space for a grand exhibition gallery on the building's entire top floor.

On December 15, 1836, tragedy struck Blodgett's Hotel, where the Patent Office was still housed. Fire, caused by ashes dumped in a wooden refuse bin in the basement, was discovered at 3 A.M. Superintendent Ellsworth, Senator Ruggles, and others rushed to the scene, but were unable to rescue anything from the building. A nearby firehouse was opened, but the leather pumping hose had disintegrated and was useless. Over 10,000 patent documents and 7,000 patent models were lost. One spectator to the scene lamented: "Poor patentees! Not a model, nor a paper, nor a book has been saved; the accumulated experience of 40 years lies smoking in ruins before me." By corresponding with patent holders, the office was able eventually to copy and restore 2,845 patents. The Patent Office relocated to temporary quarters in the District of Columbia's City Hall until the new building could be completed. The fire underscored the requirement that the new building be fireproof.

When Mills began to oversee the construction of the building in the sparsely populated capital, he had to cope with a shortage of materials and skilled labor, since another massive construction project was under way for the Treasury. He resorted to recruiting skilled masons from as far away as Philadelphia and New York. By 1838 the first floor had been finished, and the outer walls erected for much of the second and third floors. But Mills still had to cope with Elliot. The Whig Party had gained control of Congress, and Elliot, hoping to exploit his political advantage, complained that Mills was not following the building's approved design. Elliot criticized particularly Mills's curving staircase in the projecting apse, which today is considered an architectural masterpiece. Elliot also took issue with Mills's fireproof construction methods. In response, Mills expressed his "appreciation of Mr. Elliot's talents as a draughtsman," but noted that he had "no qualification to judge in the matter, having not the smallest degree of experience in building."

Senate and House congressional committees launched an investigation into Mills's vaulting system, even though none of the committee members had any expertise in building construction. Claims were levied that Mills's walls were too thin and that his vaults, if built, would collapse. Thomas U. Walter, the acclaimed architect of Girard College in Philadelphia and twenty years Mills's junior, was retained to critique Mills's design. He reported that Mills's vaults would indeed collapse unless supported by iron tie rods and interior masonry walls, rather than by the piers and columns that Mills proposed. In rebuttal Mills provided a detailed structural analysis of his design, citing his earlier buildings with the same vaulting system that had experienced no problems whatsoever. He asserted that Walter was arguing from theory instead of actual practice and that Walter's structures were frequently "overbuilt."

In good government fashion, the congressional committees retained still another architect for another opinion, the older and respected Alexander Parris from Boston. He supported Walter's findings of instability and recommended yet another vaulting system. The congressional committees unanimously recommended Mills's dismissal. After much debate, Congress permitted Mills to continue, but required him to alter his vaulting system from groin to barrel vaults and to double the number of supporting columns and piers throughout the building. This episode precipitated a six-month delay in construction and, by Mills's estimate, added $60,000 to the building's cost.

In 1840 the new Patent Office Building was ready for occupancy, although the portico was not completed until 1842. The results were magnificent indeed (fig. 13). Reached by an impressive flight of steps, the portico was graced with a double row of eight fluted Doric columns, thirty-five feet tall and six feet in diameter. Much

Fig. 13
Patent Office Building, 1846. The building's south wing, completed in 1842, dominated its neighborhood. This daguerreotype is the earliest known photographic image of the building.

of the building was devoted to open gallery space for the display of patent models, agricultural implements, historic artifacts, and scientific specimens. Offices and a library were on lower floors (fig. 14). The top floor presented the most awesome sight of all: one enormous vaulted room—266 feet long, 63 feet wide, and 30 feet high—interrupted only by rows of supporting columns. Mills claimed it was the largest exhibition hall in the United States. Commissioner Ellsworth promptly christened it the "National Gallery" (fig. 15).

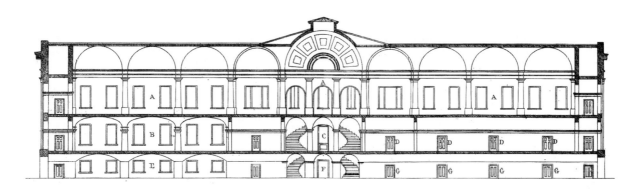

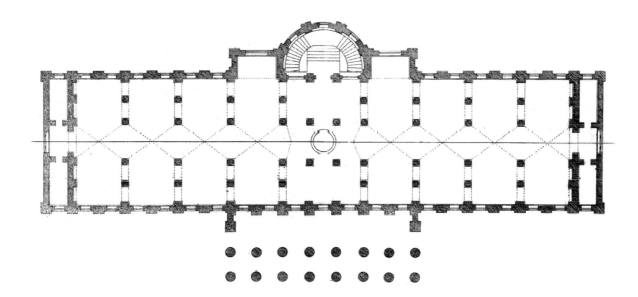

Fig. 14
Patent Office Library, 1856. The massive supporting columns of the building's second floor are clearly shown.

Fig. 15
Section and plan, 1840. More than half of the original building was to be used for exhibition space. The third-floor plan of the National Gallery shows the location of Mills's double-curving stair and the placement of supporting columns.

A Museum of Curiosities

With only seventeen employees and a limited number of patent models, the Patent Office nevertheless was soon able to fill its ample halls (fig. 16). In 1838 the U.S. Navy, under the command of Lt. Charles Wilkes, sent six ships and a dozen scientists on an exploratory expedition to the Pacific Ocean for four years. They returned with twenty tons of exotic animal, plant, mineral, and ethnographic specimens. Of the sixty-three display cases built for the National Gallery, two-thirds were filled with over 5,000 natural history objects from the Wilkes Expedition. Joining them were paintings, sculpture, artifacts, and curiosities assembled by the government-chartered National Institute and by John Varden for his Washington museum. Memorabilia of James Smithson, who bequeathed his fortune to the nation to found the Smithsonian Institution, were also placed on view. Then in 1856 the many curiosities that Commodore Matthew Perry brought back from Japan were added to the display.

Over the years, many other historical objects were donated by citizens and transferred by government agencies because the National Gallery was the largest fireproof exhibition hall in the capital. The gallery soon became known as a "museum of curiosities" and was a major tourist destination (fig. 17). On display were the original Declaration of Independence, foreign treaties bearing the signatures of kings, and the printing press that Benjamin Franklin used

Fig. 16
National Gallery of the Patent Office, 1856.
This great vaulted hall became known as a "museum of curiosities."

while a journeyman in London (fig. 18). Featured were many relics from George Washington, some donated by his family, including his commission as commander-in-chief of the Continental army; the tent, camp equipment, and sword he used during the Revolutionary War (fig. 19); and a set of Sevres china presented to Martha Washington by Lafayette. Also on display was the uniform Andrew Jackson wore at the Battle of New Orleans (fig. 20). Curiosities ranged from Egyptian and Peruvian mummies to a mosaic from Pompeii to a piece of Plymouth Rock to Davy Crockett's tomahawk to a hair from the head of Simon Bolivar. Old-master paintings (mostly copies) and portraits and busts of American presidents and statesmen, as well as 147 portraits of Indian chiefs commissioned by the War Department, were arranged around the gallery.

One curiosity on view in the building was a marble sarcophagus purportedly of the Roman emperor Alexander Severus. Commodore Jesse Elliott had brought it back from Syria on the frigate *Constitution* and presented it to Andrew Jackson "as a resting place for his remains." Jackson refused the gift, however, saying, "I cannot consent that my mortal body shall be laid in a repository prepared for an Emperor or a King—my republican feelings and principles forbid it. . . . True virtue cannot exist where pomp and parade are the governing passions."

Abraham Lincoln is the only president ever to hold a patent. He had handled patent cases while practicing law and knew how the system worked. During a trip on the Detroit River in the

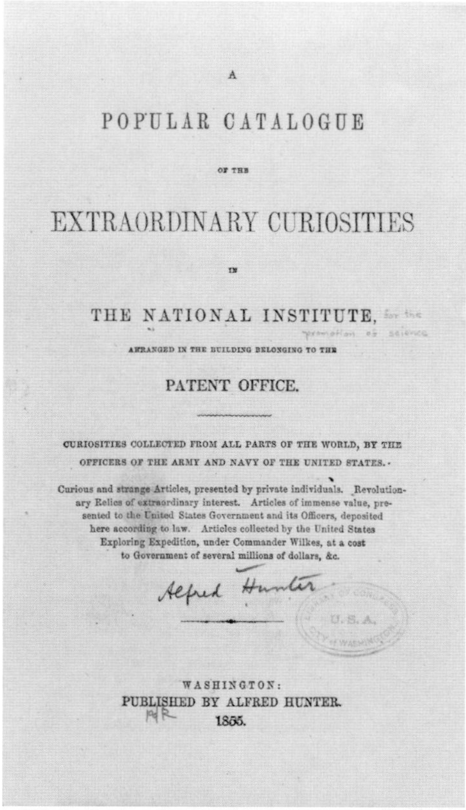

Fig. 17
Catalogue of curiosities, 1855. The catalogue described the thousands of objects on view in the National Gallery.

Fig. 18
Benjamin Franklin's printing press, 1856 illustration. It was one of the historic objects on display.

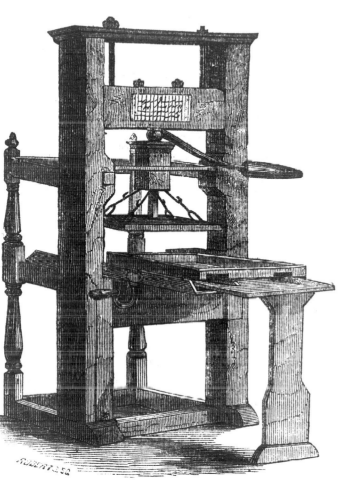

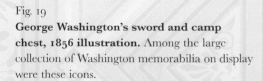

FRANKLIN'S PRESS.

Fig. 19
George Washington's sword and camp chest, 1856 illustration. Among the large collection of Washington memorabilia on display were these icons.

Fig. 20
Andrew Jackson's uniform. He wore this coat at the Battle of New Orleans in 1815.

steamboat *Globe*, he suffered a lengthy delay when the ship ran aground on sand-bars. After pondering the problem, he devised a bellows contraption for "lifting vessels over shoals," which consisted of inflatable air bags attached to a boat below the water line. A patent was issued to Lincoln in 1849, but it was never put into practical use (fig. 21). With Lincoln's subsequent rise to fame, his model became a center of attention for visitors to the Patent Office. The hat he wore at the time of his assassination was later placed on view among the National Gallery's historical artifacts.

There were by this time thousands of patent models, including some trivial ones, on display in cases in the building (fig. 22). By the 1850s, over 100,000 visitors came to the Patent Office each year to inspect the enormous range of historic, cultural, and scientific objects on view. As models poured into the building at the rate of more than 1,000 per year, the lack of exhibition space was increasingly an issue. With the completion of the Smithsonian Institution's "Castle" on the Mall, the natural history specimens, ethnographic artifacts, and James Smithson memorabilia were moved there in 1858 to make room for patent models.

Fig. 21
New and improved manner of buoying vessels over shoals, 1849, patent model replica. Abraham Lincoln is the only president to hold a patent.

Fig. 22
Patent for improved spring egg cup, 1860. This example of official "letters patent" illustrates the triviality of some of the patents granted.

No. 27.095

E PLURIBUS UNUM

The United States of America

TO ALL TO WHOM THESE LETTERS PATENT SHALL COME:

Whereas Henrietta G. Baker of Springfield Massachusetts

has alleged that she has invented a new and useful

Improved Spring Egg Cup

which she states has not been known or used before her application has
made oath that she is a Citizen of the United States
that she does verily believe that she is the original and first
inventor or discoverer of the said Egg Cup and that the same hath not to the best of her
knowledge and belief been previously known or used was paid into the treasury
of the **United States** the sum of Thirty dollars and presented a petition to the
COMMISSIONER of **PATENTS** signifying a desire of obtaining an exclusive property in the said
Egg Cup and praying that a patent may be granted for that purpose

These are Therefore to grant according
to law to the said Henrietta G. Baker her heirs administrators or
assigns for the term of fourteen years from the fourteenth day of February one thousand eight hundred
and Sixty the full and exclusive right and liberty of making constructing using and vending to
others to be used the said Egg Cup a description whereof is given in the words of the said
Henrietta G. Baker in the schedule hereunto annexed and is made a part of these presents

In Testimony whereof I have caused these Letters to be made
Patent and the Seal of the **PATENT OFFICE** has been hereunto affixed
GIVEN under my hand at the City of Washington this fourteenth
day of February in the year of our Lord one thousand eight hundred and
Sixty and of the **INDEPENDENCE** of the United States of America
the Eighty fourth

Jacob Thompson Secretary of the Interior.

S. T. Shugert Act'g Commissioner of Patents.

Era of Expansion

In 1849 the Patent Office was transferred from the State Department to the newly created Department of the Interior. Also placed under the new department were the General Land Office, Office of Indian Affairs, Pension Office, and Census Bureau. The Interior Department needed a home, and the Patent Office needed space for increased staff, expanded library, and 17,000 patent models now overflowing its premises. To meet the need, Congress that same year appropriated $50,000 from the patent fund in the Treasury to begin work on the foundations for the east and west wings (fig. 23) in accordance with William Elliot's 1836 plan of four wings around an open courtyard (fig. 24). Robert Mills was retained as architect and would report to the secretary of the interior. The commissioner of public buildings, who also reported to the Interior secretary, would approve contracting and payment arrangements.

With an additional appropriation from Congress of $103,000, work could proceed on the east wing, but further construction on the west wing had to be postponed until sufficient funding was authorized. Mills's insistence on white marble from Maryland quarries for the exterior walls and granite for the interior courtyard walls was accepted without challenge. Also approved was his proposal to paint the brown Aquia Creek sandstone of the original south wing to match the white marble. The first and second floors of the east wing were to be offices for the

Fig. 23
Patent Office Building, ca. 1857. This view was composed shortly after the east wing (with portico at right) and west wing (projecting at far left) were completed in white marble. The brown sandstone of the original, or south, wing (with portico at left) was painted white to match.

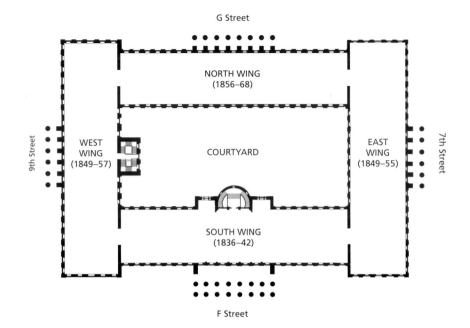

G Street

NORTH WING
(1856–68)

WEST
WING
(1849–57)

COURTYARD

EAST
WING
(1849–55)

9th Street

7th Street

SOUTH WING
(1836–42)

F Street

Interior Department, and the third floor was to be another grand open hall for the display of patent models. By the end of 1850, the first two floors were completed.

Then the troubles began that would end Mills's professional career as an architect. President Zachary Taylor died in office in 1850 (fig. 25) and was succeeded by Vice President Millard Fillmore. Awaiting Fillmore when he took office was a letter from William Elliot complaining that Mills was "destroying the original plan" for the Patent Office Building. Others levied false charges that Mills had used inferior materials and had overpaid contractors. A year later, William Easby, a longtime Whig, was appointed commissioner of public buildings and with Elliot's assistance set out to get rid of Mills. During earlier business ventures, Easby had bid unsuccessfully for stone, sand, and lime contracts for the Patent Office construction. Furthermore, Mills, who had won the competition for the Washington Monument and was supervising its construction, rejected stone that Easby supplied because of its inferior quality.

Revenge was the order of the day. Easby appointed a committee of three private citizens, including William Elliot, to investigate materials, payments,

Fig. 24
Schematic plan. This plan of the building shows the sequence of construction for each wing.

Fig. 25
South façade, 1850. The columns are draped in black for the death of President Zachary Taylor.

and adherence to plans in Mills's handling of the construction. Based on the committee's findings, Easby charged Mills with incompetence and recommended his dismissal. To further his case, Easby appointed yet another committee of three architects, including Mills's rival Thomas U. Walter. Earlier Mills had entered the architectural competition for the addition of the new House and Senate wings of the U.S. Capitol, but lost to Walter. It was a replay of the 1838 investigation of Mills's work on the south wing. At the request of the secretary of the interior, however, a team from the Army Corps of Engineers examined Mills's proposed groin vaulting system and found it perfectly sound. Easby nevertheless proceeded with his investigation. He presented to the secretary selected and misleading documents that ostensibly demonstrated Mills had, on occasion, not awarded bids to the lowest bidder and had committed other offenses. In July 1851, Mills was dismissed, and Walter was appointed to the position of architect.

Mills then began a two-year campaign to regain his position. He provided complete, rather than selective, documentation and a point-by-point rebuttal in an appeal to the secretary of the interior. He appealed to Congress. He appealed to his old friend Jefferson Davis, who was then secretary of war. He appealed to Franklin Pierce, who in 1853 had succeeded Fillmore as president. All to no avail. Work on the Washington Monument had been suspended for lack of funds. Mills was then seventy-two years old. He died in Washington in 1855 in financial straits. In an ironic twist of fate, William Elliot had died a year earlier at age forty-seven before the completion of his one and only building that was actually constructed.

Despite his past disagreements with Mills, Thomas Ustick Walter was eminently qualified to undertake construction and further design of the Patent Office Building (fig. 26). The son of a brick mason, Walter was born in Philadelphia in 1804. At fifteen, he began an apprenticeship with the noted Philadelphia architect William Strickland. Walter set up his own practice in 1830, and three years later was awarded the commission to design and construct Girard College, an orphanage in Philadelphia endowed by Stephen Girard, then the richest man in the United States. The trustees of the college sent Walter to Europe to study the best and latest examples of architecture in preparation for his forthcoming work. When completed in 1847, Girard College

Fig. 26
Thomas U. Walter, ca. 1851. He was the supervising architect of the Patent Office Building from 1851 to 1865.

was acclaimed by some as "the finest specimen of classic architecture on this continent."

After winning the competition for the extensions of the U.S. Capitol, Walter moved with his family to Washington, where he not only worked on the Capitol and the Patent Office but also on the Treasury and the Post Office Department buildings that Mills had begun. He was a founder of the American Institute of Architects in 1857 and its president for ten years. In 1858 he was awarded an honorary doctorate by Harvard. He died in Philadelphia in 1887.

When Walter took charge, construction of the east wing of the Patent Office had reached the roof line. Edward Clark, a young architect whom Walter brought with him from Philadelphia, was appointed his assistant to perform day-to-day operations on-site, allowing Walter to pursue his duties at the Capitol. Walter, ever cautious, decided to leave the temporary tie rods across Mills's arches on the third floor in place, although they should have been removed after the mortar in the brick vaults had set. They remain there today. Nevertheless, the magnificent third floor—now called the Lincoln Gallery—exemplified Mills's groined vaulting system supported by two rows of marble pillars, which was the very system Mills had envisioned for his National Gallery in the south wing (fig. 27). Today the Lincoln Gallery stands as a fitting tribute to Mills's architectural genius, a soaring cathedral-like space—271 feet long, 64 feet wide, and 30 feet high.

The east wing was completed in 1853, except for its portico, which was not finished until 1855 (see fig. 23). The portico of six monumental Doric columns was not in Elliot's 1836 plan of the building, but was designed by Walter to match the portico on the south façade. The new wing boasted the most modern of conveniences: gas lighting, hot-air heat from furnaces in the basement, hot-and-cold

running water piped to marble basins, and even a plant for sterilizing cuspidors.

With an appropriation of $150,000, work on the west wing resumed in 1852 and proceeded rapidly. Here, too, the top floor would be an enormous open space for the display of patent models. However, Walter employed a new structural system there of iron beams and trusses in the attic to support the roof and suspend the model hall's coffered ceiling, which, unlike Mills's masonry vaults, was not fireproof. Thus this great hall, equal in size to the east wing's Lincoln Gallery, was entirely open and needed no supporting columns or piers that would obstruct the view. For the west wing's first and second floors, Walter avoided a series of constricting, weight-bearing walls by using a system of barrel vaults supported on piers. By 1857 the west wing, with its portico of six Doric columns, was completed.

Because of the rapid growth in the number of patent models—almost 25,000 by 1853—the Patent Office Building needed an extensive system of display cases in both east and west wing galleries. Walter designed modular cases constructed of cast iron, wood, and glass in two tiers. The upper tier would be reached by internal iron stairways. Costing $110,000 and requiring twenty-four tons of iron to build, the cases would be arranged on either side of a central aisle running the length of the gallery (fig. 28). Three years were required to catalogue and place the models within the cases.

Fig. 27
East model room (Lincoln Gallery), 1856. The vaulting system that Mills designed soars above the patent model cases arranged on two levels.

Fig. 28
West model room, ca. 1870. The flat ceiling illustrates the new construction system of the west and north wings that required no supporting columns.

One of the more colorful figures associated with the Patent Office about this time was Clara Barton (fig. 29). A schoolteacher from Massachusetts, she came to Washington in 1854. Recognizing her talent for organization, patent commissioner Charles Mason hired her as his confidential clerk at an annual salary of $1,400. As such, she became the first woman ever employed in a regular position with the U.S. government at wages equal to those of a man. Over the years, women had worked for the Patent Office as copyists of patent applications and correspondence, but they worked at home on a piecemeal basis at the rate of ten cents per hundred words. By 1865, fifty-three women who had worked at home were converted to employees at the Patent Office at an annual salary of $700, but they were crammed into six rooms under abysmal working conditions.

Needless to say, Clara Barton suffered the resentment of male employees, who were habitually rude to her. They blew cigar smoke in her face, spat tobacco juice at her, and cast aspersions on her morality, but she remarked in a letter, "Any blow that they could slanderously aim at me in *these* days would make about as much impression upon me a[s] a sling shot would upon the hide of a Shark—I have got above them." During a three-month absence of Commissioner Mason, the secretary of the interior, who opposed women working in government offices, dismissed Barton, but Mason reinstated her in a temporary position when he returned. Barton went on to tend wounded soldiers in the Patent Office Building in 1861 and then to organize heroic, life-saving medical care for the wounded on Civil War battlefields. She is best known for founding the American Red Cross in 1881 and serving as its first president until 1904.

In 1856 construction began on the north wing of the Patent Office with an initial appropriation of $200,000. Walter employed the same structural system for its

Fig. 29
Clara Barton, ca. 1865. She was employed as a clerk in the Patent Office at wages equal to those of a man and later founded the American Red Cross.

third-floor exhibition gallery as he had for the west wing's model hall, producing a grand unobstructed room, 266 feet long, 60 feet wide, and 30 feet high. For the first and second floors, however, he used a new system of shallow brick vaults supported by horizontal iron I-beams that rested on masonry walls. These two floors were arranged, as in the east wing, as individual offices opening onto a spacious central corridor. By the outbreak of the Civil War, the north wing was completed, except for the eight-columned portico and interior finishing of the third-floor exhibition hall. Work was suspended during the war, but plastering, painting, and laying of the marble floor continued sporadically on the top floor.

SLEEPING-BUNKS OF THE FIRST RHODE ISLAND REGIMENT, AT THE PATENT OFFICE, WASHINGTON.
[SKETCHED BY OUR SPECIAL ARTIST.]

The Civil War Years

The election of Abraham Lincoln in November 1860 transformed the American political landscape. Gone was the series of northern democratic presidents and their policy of accommodating the South. The new Republican Party had been born. Tensions escalated between North and South. In December, South Carolina seceded from the Union, followed in early 1861 by six other southern states. Federal property was seized by the rebel states. So great was the fear of assassination attempts on the new president that Lincoln was persuaded to arrive in Washington for his inauguration in secret at 6 A.M., rather than in the afternoon when welcoming ceremonies were planned. In April, Fort Sumter was attacked and captured by the rebels, and war was declared. State militia throughout the North were mobilized, and Lincoln issued a call for 75,000 volunteers for the army. The nation's capital, however, was totally unprepared for war.

As troops poured into Washington, they were billeted temporarily in the Rotunda of the Capitol and other government buildings. In April and May, the First Rhode Island Regiment was quartered in the west wing model hall of the Patent Office Building (fig. 30). The unit was commanded by Colonel Ambrose E. Burnside, a West Point graduate who cut a striking figure with his luxuriant whiskers (fig. 31). Accompanying his troop were a laundress and three young female relatives who "utterly refused to be left at home." The regiment eventually

Fig. 30
Soldiers' sleeping bunks, 1861. After being temporarily quartered in the Patent Office, the First Rhode Island Regiment left behind 400 broken panes in model cases.

moved out to an encampment, leaving behind 400 broken panes in the cases and absconding with a number of patent models.

With the battles of Manassas, Antietam, and Fredericksburg, casualties arrived in the nation's capital in ever-increasing numbers. One thousand beds were set up—then another 2,000—in the building's east, west, and north exhibition galleries. The Patent Office Building served as a military hospital from September 1861 to April 1863, by which time other facilities had been constructed for the wounded. President and Mrs. Lincoln visited the sick and wounded soldiers in the building. Another more frequent visitor was the poet Walt Whitman (fig. 32).

Whitman had published his first edition of *Leaves of Grass* in 1855, but it sold few copies. He worked as a carpenter, schoolteacher, and newspaper editor and contributor, but his financial situation was always precarious. Seeking employment, Whitman moved to Washington in 1863, but at age forty-three found only part-time work as a copyist. His attention soon turned to the wounded. As he wrote to friends and newspapers about his hospital visits, people began to send him money. During regular trips to the Patent Office, he brought small gifts of food, pens and paper,

Fig. 31
First Rhode Island Regiment, 1861 (detail). Colonel Ambrose E. Burnside, center, his arm propped against a tree, later commanded the Army of the Potomac.

Fig. 32
Walt Whitman, ca. 1867. He tended wounded soldiers hospitalized in the Patent Office Building during the Civil War.

even money, which he dispensed carefully (fig. 33). He wrote letters for patients, read to them, and played games with them. This account survives from his diary of 1863:

A few weeks ago the vast area . . . of that noblest of Washington buildings was crowded close with rows of sick, badly wounded and dying soldiers. . . . I went there many times. It was a strange, solemn, and . . . fascinating sight. . . . Two of the immense apartments are fill'd with high and ponderous glass cases, crowded with models in miniature of every kind of . . . invention, it ever enter'd into the mind of man to conceive . . . It was, indeed, a curious scene, especially at night when lit up. The glass cases, the beds, the forms lying there, the gallery above, the marble pave-ment under foot—the suffering, and the fortitude to bear it . . . such were the sights but lately in the Patent-office.

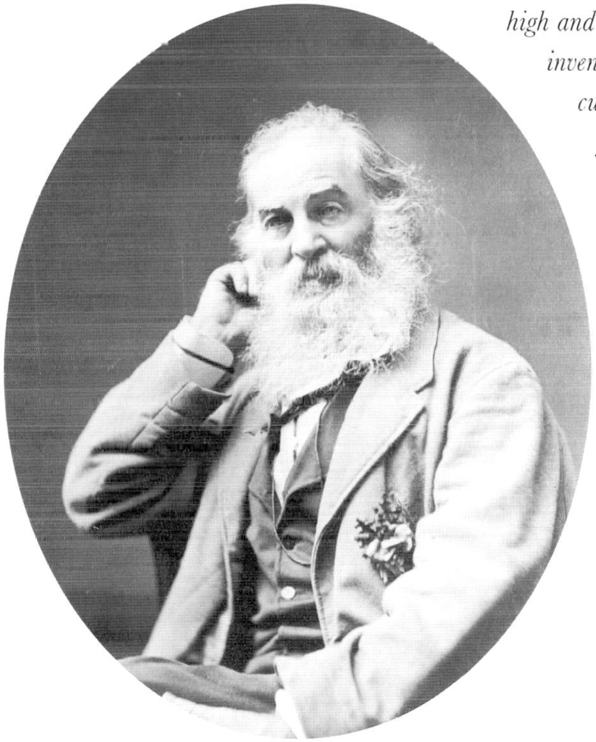

During its use as a barracks and hospital, the Patent Office continued its customary operations, although the number of patent applications declined substantially during the war.

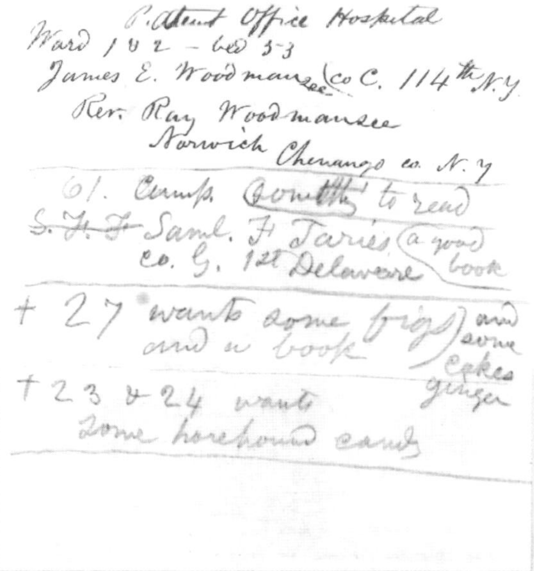

Patent Office Hospital
Ward 1 & 2 – bed 53
James E. Woodmansee co C. 114th N.Y
Rev. Ray Woodmansee
Norwich Chenango co. N.Y
61. Cump. Something to read
S. H. F. Saml. F. Jarvis (a good book)
co. G. 1st Delaware
+ 27 wants some figs and a book (and some cakes ginger)
+ 23 & 24 wants some horehound candy

Fig. 33
Walt Whitman's memorandum, 1862.
Whitman noted requests received from the wounded. The men in beds #23 and #24, for instance, asked for horehound candy.

Lincoln's Inaugural Ball

Arguably the single most dramatic historic event to take place in the Patent Office Building was the ball held on the evening of March 6, 1865, for Abraham Lincoln's second inauguration. Lincoln's decisive defeat of Democrat George McClellan for a second term ensured that the Union army would aggressively pursue the Civil War. It was now nearing its conclusion, and victory was clearly in sight. Lincoln authorized an inaugural celebration with no expense spared. The ideal location for the ball was the vast empty hall on the top floor of the Patent Office Building's nearly completed north wing.

Engraved invitations were issued to officials and dignitaries (fig. 34), and tickets were sold to the public for ten dollars that admitted a gentleman and two ladies. Proceeds from the sales benefited the families of soldiers in the field. The great north hall was draped with American flags, and a dais was erected with blue-and-gold sofas to accommodate the presidential party. Gas lighting was provided by overhead pipes suspended from the ceiling. Walt Whitman, who had finally procured a clerkship in the Bureau of Indian Affairs in the Patent Office Building, was eager to inspect the halls being prepared for the inaugural festivities. He offered this reflection:

I have been up to look at the dance and supper rooms, for the inauguration ball, at the Patent office; and I could not help thinking, what a different scene they presented to my view since, fill'd

Lincoln's inaugural ball, March 6, 1865
(detail; see fig. 37, p. 56). The building's enormous and unobstructed north hall was ideal for dancing for the 4,000 guests. The band is on the raised platform at left.

with a crowded mass of the worst wounded of the war, brought in from second Bull Run, Antietam, and Fredericksburgh. To-night, beautiful women, perfumes, the violins' sweetness, the polka and the waltz; then the amputation, the blue face, the groan, the glassy eye of the dying, the clotted rag, the odor of wounds and blood, and many a mother's son amid strangers, passing away untended.

Arriving guests made their way up the great stairway to the entrance on the south portico and then to the third floor, which opened onto the other three great halls. A band performed in each hall: promenade music for the east gallery, dance music for the north hall, and dinner music for the west wing. President and Mrs. Lincoln (figs. 35 and 36) arrived at 10:30 P.M. and were escorted to their dais in the north gallery. The *New-York Times* described the president as "trying to throw off care for a while, but with rather ill success; yet he seemed pleased and gratified, as he was greeted by the people." Mrs. Lincoln was resplendent in costly white satin with a lace shawl and a fan trimmed in ermine

Fig. 34
Invitation to inaugural ball, 1865. This particular invitation was issued to Clara Barton, who kept it as a memento.

and silver spangles. Lincoln was dressed in a plain black suit and white kid gloves. The promenading and dancing proceeded until midnight (fig. 37), when an elaborate supper was served in the west hall among the patent model cases.

The buffet table stretched 250 feet in length and was decorated with enormous confectionery models, with one of the U.S. Capitol forming the centerpiece. Among

Fig. 35
Abraham Lincoln, 1864. This photograph by Mathew Brady was taken the year before the ball.

Fig. 36
Mary Todd Lincoln, ca. 1863 (detail). Her extravagance in clothes was well publicized at the time. Her gown for the ball was white, but more elaborate than the one depicted here.

Fig. 37
Lincoln's inaugural ball, March 6, 1865.
Dancing continued until 4 a.m., and by dawn
all of the guests had departed.

Fig. 38
Bill of fare for the ball, 1865. The buffet
table was lavish, but in the onslaught much of
the food was trampled underfoot.

the gastronomic offerings were oyster and terrapin stews, beef à l'anglais, veal Malakoff, turkeys, pheasants, quail, venison, ducks, hams, and lobsters, and ornamental pyramids of desserts, cakes, and ice cream (fig. 38). By midnight there were more than 4,000 guests, but the buffet table, placed in a corridor only twenty feet wide between model cases, was designed to serve only 300 people at a time.

When supper was announced, a mob rushed to the buffet. Chaos ensued. Foraging gentlemen grabbed large platters of food to carry to their guests, spilling much of it on the surging crowd. Glasses were smashed as waiters rushed in fresh supplies of delicacies. The next day, a newspaper account described the scene, "In less than an hour the table was a wreck. . . . positively frightful to behold." Another newspaper reported, "The floor of the supper room was soon sticky, pasty and oily with wasted confections, mashed cake, and debris of fowl and meat." It was alleged that as much food was wasted as was consumed. The president and first lady departed at 1:30, but dancing continued until 4 A.M. A month later, Lincoln was dead, felled by an assassin's bullet at Ford's Theatre, a block from the Patent Office.

BILL OF FARE
OF THE
Presidential Inauguration Ball
IN THE
CITY OF WASHINGTON, D. C.,
On the 6th of March 1865.

Oyster Stews . . . .
Terrapin " . . . .
Oysters, pickled . . . .

BEEF.
Roast Beef . . . .
Filet de Beef . . . .
Beef à-la-mode . . . .
Beef à l'anglais . . . .

VEAL.
Leg of Veal . . . .
Fricandeau . . . .
Veal Malakoff . . . .

POULTRY.
Roast Turkey . . . .
Boned "
Roast Chicken . . . .
Grouse, boned and roast . . . . .

GAME.
Pheasant . . . .
Quail . . . .
Venison . . . .

PATETES.
Patète of Duck en gelée . . . . .
Patète de fois gras . . . . .

SMOKED.
Ham . . . .
Tongue en gelée . . . .
      do   plain . . . .

SALADES.
Chicken . . . .
Lobster . . . .

Ornamental Pyramides.
Nougate . . . .
Orange . . . .
Caramel with Fancy Cream Candy
Cocoanut . . . .
Macaroon . . . .

Croquant . . . .
Chocolate . . . .
Tree Cakes . . . .

CAKES AND TARTS.
Almond Sponge . . . .
Belle Alliance . . . .
Dame Blanche . . . .
Macaroon Tart . . . .
Tart à la Nelson . . . .
Tarte à l'Orleans . . . .
      do   à la Portugaise . . . .
      do   à la Vienne . . . .
Pound Cake . . . .
Sponge Cake . . . .
Lady Cake . . . .
Fancy small Cakes . . . .

JELLIES AND CREAMS.
Calfsfoot and Wine Jelly . . . . .
Charlotte à la Russe . . . .
      do   do   Vanilla . . . .
Blanc Mangue . . . .
Crème Neapolitane . . . .
      do   à la Nelson . . . .
      do   Chateaubriand . . . . . .
      do   à la Smyrna . . . .
      do   do   Nesselrode . . . . . .
Bombe à la Vanilla . . . .

ICE CREAM.
Vanilla . . . .
Lemon . . . .
White Coffee . . . .
Chocolate . . . .
Burnt Almonds . . . .
Maraschino . . . .

FRUIT ICES.
Strawberry . . . .
Orange . . . .
Lemon . . . .

DESSERT.
Grapes, Almonds, Raisins, &c.

Coffee and Chocolate.

Furnished by **G. A. BALZER,** CONFECTIONER,
Cor. 9th & D Sts., Washington, D. C.

Completion of the Building

After the Civil War, difficulties arose when work resumed on the north wing. The marble quarries in Maryland had flooded and needed to be drained before construction could commence. Thomas U. Walter resigned as architect of the Capitol in 1865 over political meddling and a contract dispute and returned to Philadelphia. His assistant Edward Clark succeeded him in carrying out Walter's design to completion (fig. 39). Clark at the same time was appointed architect of the Capitol. By 1868 the eight-columned north portico and steps were finally finished (fig. 40), and the cases for patent models were installed in the great room where Lincoln's inaugural ball had been held (fig. 41). The same fabrication and configuration of cases in the west wing were employed for those in the north wing.

At the time of its completion, the Patent Office Building was the largest office building in the United States, covering 333,000 square feet with 588 windows on two city blocks. The great third-floor galleries in the four wings formed a continuous exhibition space of 1,062 feet—or almost one-quarter of a mile—in circumference (fig. 42). Construction costs for the building over thirty-two years totaled $2,347,011. With its four Greek porticoes of monumental proportions, the Patent Office Building for decades was the dominant feature of its neighborhood (see fig. 39).

With the end of the Civil War, patent applications and their accompanying models increased exponentially at the rate of 20–40 percent each year (see frontispiece, patent

Fig. 39
**Bird's-Eye View of the City of Washington,
1862** (detail). The Patent Office Building is
at the bottom right, with the Smithsonian
Castle above and the Washington Monument
to its right.

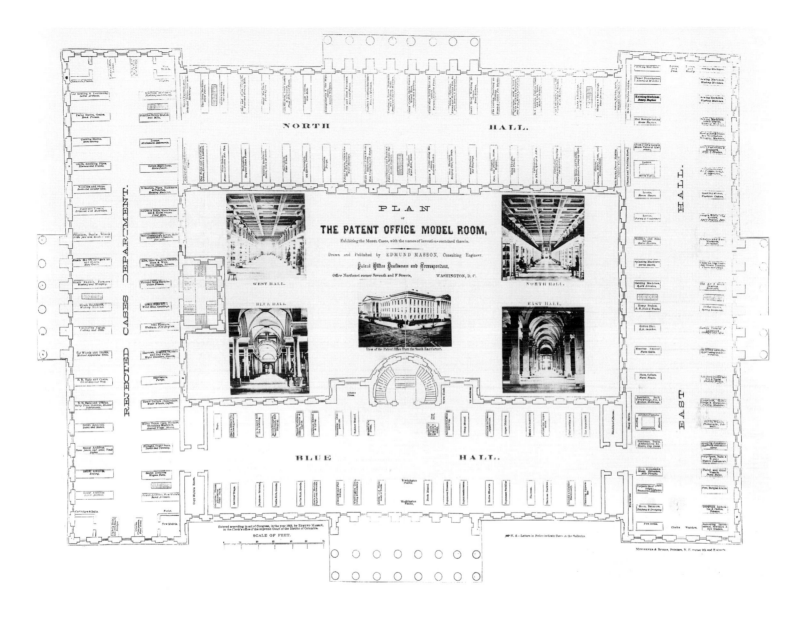

Fig. 40
View of north façade, 1870s. The portico terminated the vista down Eighth Street.

Fig. 41
North model room, ca. 1875. This room was the site of Lincoln's second inaugural ball.

Fig. 42
Plan of top-floor model halls, 1868. The four great interconnecting galleries stretched almost one-quarter of a mile in circumference and eventually displayed more than 200,000 models crowded into cases almost nine feet tall.

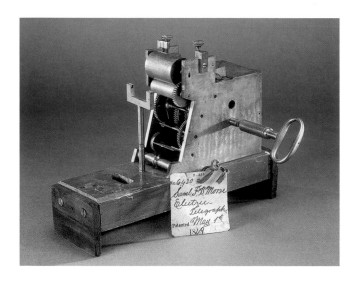

examiners at work). One patent applicant went so far as to submit an embalmed baby as his model for an improved embalming process; it was rejected. Among the notable patents granted during the century were Samuel F. B. Morse's telegraph of 1849 (fig. 43), Isaac M. Singer's sewing machine of 1851, John Henry Belter's laminated chair of 1858 (fig. 44), and Alexander Graham Bell's telephone of 1876 (fig. 45). Embellishments of patents could become quite fanciful, as exemplified by David Clark's sewing machine of 1858 (fig. 46).

By 1877 the display cases were filled with more than 200,000 models, each no larger than one cubic foot, crammed into cases almost nine feet high. The models were grouped by subject to facilitate finding any field of interest. Such a concentration of small models, by far the largest in the world, presented a mind-boggling spectacle to the visiting public.

During the 1870s, Washington underwent a radical transformation into a modern city. Under a new territorial form of municipal government, an extensive sewer system was installed, parks were laid out, 3,000 street lamps were erected, 60,000 trees were planted, and 119 miles of streets were graded and paved. The grade of the streets around the Patent Office Building was lowered, even as much as twelve feet along the south and east sides, necessitating a change in the steps leading to the south and east porticoes. The east steps could be extended, but the lower section of the south steps was truncated by a wall, transforming the steps into two side flights of stairs (fig. 47). Additional changes to the building included the handsome cast-iron fence,

Fig. 43
Samuel F. B. Morse's telegraph, 1849. This patent model and the others illustrated here were on display in the model halls. A well-known artist, Morse turned inventor in a time of financial hardship.

Fig. 44
John Henry Belter's chair, 1858. His patent was for a method of producing laminated furniture in two curves.

Fig. 45
Alexander Graham Bell's telephone, 1876.
Bell's telephone, which worked only over short
distances, was quickly improved by others,
including Thomas Edison.

Fig. 46
David Clark's sewing machine, 1858. Sewing
machines could become quite whimsical.

still in place today, which was erected around the entire perimeter of the property. There were also changes in the painted decoration of the interior rooms (fig. 48). The south wing's National Gallery was painted blue and became known as the Blue Hall.

Following the Civil War, Washington boomed. Its population increased from 109,000 in 1870 to 232,745 by 1900. Seventh Street, along the east side of the Patent Office Building, became the principal downtown retail shopping corridor. A streetcar line to the suburbs ran down the center of the street. A small army of patent attorneys, agents, draftsmen, and model makers to serve the ever-increasing number of patent applicants grew up around the Patent Office. It was a vibrant neighborhood (fig. 49).

Fig. 47
South portico, ca. 1900. The lowered street level required a reconfiguration of the entrance stairs.

Fig. 48
South wing lobby, ca. 1879. Painted decoration and Victorian lighting fixtures were added to the building during the later nineteenth century. At the rear is the double-curving stair that Mills designed.

Fig. 49
Neighborhood business district, ca. 1910.
The streets around the Patent Office Building
became a lively commercial area after the
Civil War.

The Conflagration

"Fire!" The cry rang throughout the Patent Office Building at 11 A.M. on September 24, 1877 (fig. 50). A later investigation by an official board of inquiry found that copyists on the first floor of the west wing had complained of the cold, so a workman obligingly started a fire in a grate and set up a blower to fan the flames. Sparks from the fire traveled up a flue and spewed onto the building's roof, igniting a series of wide wooden grates placed over gutters to protect them from debris. Although some of the internal struts supporting the roof were iron, the roof's copper sheathing was laid over 100,000 board feet of pine planking. The fire soon ate through the copper to the pine boards and then spread to the 12,000 rejected patent models and other flammable material stored on wooden shelving in the attic. Beneath the attic was the coffered ceiling of the great model hall, which was also constructed of wood.

The fire spread rapidly, aggravated by a brisk wind from the south that fed the flames. Soon the north wing, constructed like the west wing, was engulfed. The burning roofs and ceilings collapsed into the exhibition halls below, smashing the cases and igniting the models. Firemen rushed to the scene, but the fire on the roof was eighty feet above the street, which was higher than the water pressure from the hydrants could reach. Water pumped from fire wagons through

Fig. 50
Fire at the Patent Office Building, September 24, 1877. Water pressure from hydrants was inadequate to reach the burning roof. A large crowd gathered to watch the conflagration.

hoses proved woefully inadequate for so massive a blaze. Baltimore shipped four fire engines by rail to Washington, which were then drawn by horses to the fire. An estimated 5,000 spectators crowded the streets to witness the conflagration. Patrols of mounted police were called to keep order.

Employees frantically began to transport patent models, drawings, and important historic artifacts from the burning building (figs. 51 and 52). Fortunately, brigades of rescuers were able to spirit to safety 777 folios containing 211,243 original patent drawings. Others inside the building prevented the spread of the fire by plugging ventilation shafts spewing live coals and molten metal. The rejected models in the attic were destroyed, which was no great loss, but 114,000 models in the west and north halls were damaged. Of this number, 87,000 were irretrievably lost, but 27,000 were eventually salvaged and restored (fig. 53). By midafternoon it was all over (fig. 54). All except 300 of the original

Fig. 51
Bringing down the models. Employees and others helped to rescue models and documents from the fire.

Fig. 52
Attempting to rescue the Franklin press. Every effort was made to save the historic artifacts in the building.

patent drawings escaped the fire or were carried to safety. The salvaged models were painstakingly bathed in sulfuric acid to remove rust and dirt, then washed in lime water to counteract the acid, and finally dried in sawdust. Machinists used the corresponding drawing for each model to fabricate missing parts and straighten bent members.

The south and east wings designed by Robert Mills survived the fire undamaged, even though their roofs were constructed of the same sheet copper over pine planking as the roofs that burned. These wings' survival was due primarily to the interior masonry walls that extended through the attics and separated them from the burned wings. The efforts of the firefighters and the strong wind blowing away from these wings also played an important part in containing the fire. Nor did the fire penetrate to the building's second floor, since the marble pavers of the third-floor model halls and the masonry support beneath them acted as a fire barrier for the office levels below.

Fig. 53
Salvaging models. As many models as possible were sorted, cleaned, and restored after the fire.

Fig. 54
West model hall after the fire, September 25, 1877. The fire destroyed the top floors of the west and north wings, as well as 87,000 patent models.

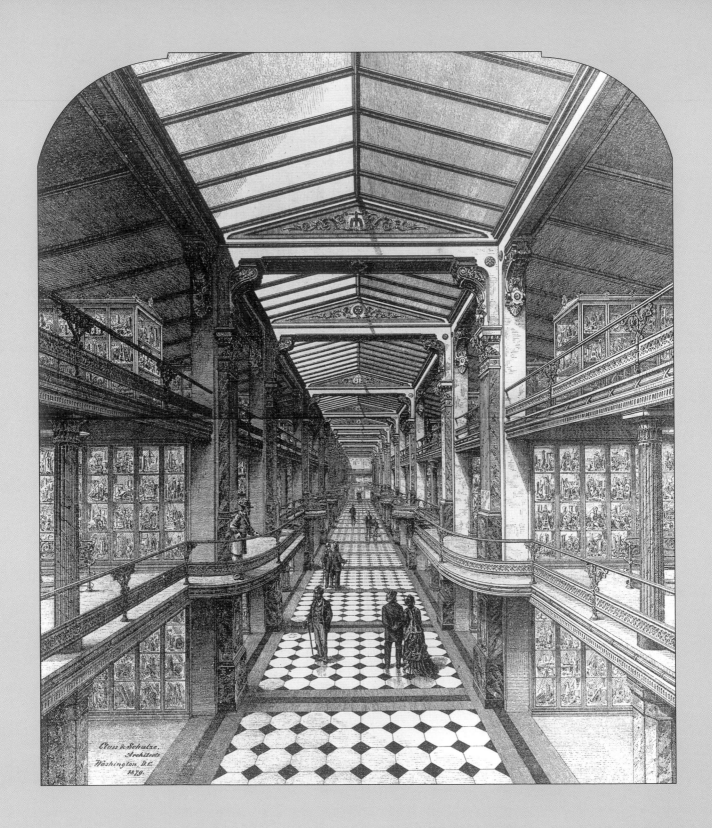

Cluss & Schulze.
Architects
Washington, D.C.
1879.

Rebuilding

A board of survey was appointed to investigate the fire damage to the building and offer advice for reconstruction. It recommended that the west and north wings be rebuilt using the best fireproof materials and techniques (fig. 55). To alleviate the overcrowded office conditions, the board proposed the addition of a fourth attic story on all four wings and construction of a three-story passageway across the center of the courtyard to improve circulation between the north and south wings. In response, Congress essentially adopted these recommendations and in 1878 authorized a national architectural competition for a suitable design, the winner to receive a $600 prize. The contest stipulated that the building be reconstructed "substantially as it stood before the fire." The addition of a fourth floor would be permitted if it did not detract from the structure's "monumental character."

The thirteen entries submitted in the competition were judged by a "committee of experts." The winner was Josse A. Vrydagh of Terre Haute, Indiana, an architect unknown on the national scene. His submission, however, did meet the specifications of the competition, including a fourth attic story and a connecting wing across the courtyard. Critics immediately raised objections to the proposed additions, however, and Vrydagh's plan failed to win essential political support.

Fig. 55
Rebuilt west model hall, 1879. Construction was fireproof. A new skylight provided much-needed light.

The local architect Adolf Cluss (fig. 56) had been a member of the board of survey and had himself submitted a design in the competition. He did have the necessary political connections, but he also had a secret past. Born in Germany in 1825 of a paternal lineage of master builders, Cluss was trained as an engineer and architect. As a young man, he became an ardent communist. He first met Karl Marx in Brussels, rose to secretary of the Communist League in Mainz, and represented workers as a leader in the Revolution of 1848. With the revolution's collapse, he emigrated to Washington and for the next twenty years held various governmental positions as an engineer or architect. Although concealing his communist sympathies, he corresponded for ten years, sometimes weekly, with Marx, Frederick Engels, and other European leaders of the communist movement. He also wrote articles for German-American newspapers and helped organize workers' meetings. Marx said of him, "Cluss is one of our best and most talented people." By 1858 Cluss had become disenchanted with communism and decided to break with Marx. His marriage in 1859 and start of a family undoubtedly influenced his decision.

After establishing a private practice, Cluss designed a series of important buildings in Washington, including innovative public schools that

Fig. 56
Adolf Cluss, 1880 (detail). He was the architect responsible for reconstructing the Patent Office Building after the fire of 1877.

earned international acclaim, large public markets, churches, residences, a Masonic hall, and most prominently the now-demolished Agriculture Department Building on the Mall. His designs were contemporary for their time, in popular Victorian styles. From 1878 to 1881, he was involved with the design and construction of the Smithsonian's National Museum Building (now the Arts and Industries Building), adjacent to the Smithsonian's Castle. So it was not surprising that he secured the commission to rebuild the west and north wings of the Patent Office Building without additions.

Employing the latest technologically fireproof materials, Cluss and his partner Paul Schulze in 1879 began reconstructing the third-floor model halls in three tiers supported by a double row of piers with a skylight above the central aisle; on either side of the aisle were patent models in cases (see fig. 55). No wood was used in the construction, except for the outside window sash, and new model cases were made entirely of wrought iron. "Modern Renaissance" was the term used at the time to describe Cluss's Victorian decorative scheme. His colorful faux marble finishes, detailed bronze railings, and elaborate columns (fig. 57) presented a vivid contrast to the austere

Fig. 57
Column capital. Cluss's Victorian decoration was described at the time as "modern Renaissance."

classical design of Mills and Walter. Cluss finished his work on the two wings in 1881, at a cost of $246,000.

Cluss repeatedly pressed for the renovation of the south and east wings in the same fireproof construction he used for the other wings. He focused on the great hall of the south wing, Mills's National Gallery, which, he said, suffered a leaky roof, rotting woodwork, and falling plaster. Finally, Congress in 1883 appropriated funds only for the south wing, fortunately leaving the east wing's Lincoln Gallery intact. Cluss could have replaced only the wooden attic and roof of the south wing above Mills's fireproof masonry vaults. Instead, he gutted the entire top-floor hall and rebuilt it in the same exuberant style of the west and north wings.

The first level of the new south hall, later referred to as the "Great Hall," was designed for much-needed offices, rather than models. In the center of the hall was an enormous foyer that rose forty feet to an octagonal stained-glass dome twenty feet in diameter (fig. 58). Medallion plaster portraits of inventors Benjamin Franklin, Thomas Jefferson, Eli Whitney, and Robert Fulton were set into the walls. The lower section of the hall was decorated with black, red, and green marble wainscoting. The floor was paved in colorful encaustic tiles in the style of Minton, but they were actually manufactured by the short-lived United States Encaustic Tile Works of Indianapolis. Work on the south wing was completed in 1885 at a cost of $171,000. Cluss retired from his practice in 1890 and died in Washington fifteen years later.

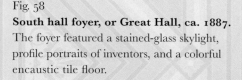

Fig. 58
South hall foyer, or Great Hall, ca. 1887.
The foyer featured a stained-glass skylight, profile portraits of inventors, and a colorful encaustic tile floor.

Decline

Gradually, the character and aura of the monumental structure began to change. In the late nineteenth century, the Patent Office Building needed ever more space for government offices and storage (fig. 59). The flood of patent applications continued unabated in the 1880s and 1890s, reaching 250,000 a year by the turn of the century. The patent staff grew to accommodate the demand. In addition, the Department of the Interior added staff as it expanded to include the U.S. Geological Survey, Bureau of Education, Bureau of Labor, and Bureau of Mines, and jurisdiction over U.S. territories and thirteen national parks. Eventually the building was bursting at its seams. At the same time, the Patent Office Building was deprived of much of its interest as a tourist attraction. In 1883 the remaining historical artifacts, portraits, and artworks from the former National Gallery were sent to the Smithsonian's National Museum Building following its completion.

One fortuitous event occurred during this era, however, when the Remington typewriter was patented in 1878, a radical improvement over Hansen's 1872 model (figs. 60 and 61). The patent commissioner instantly recognized that the new machine would revolutionize the way business was conducted and ordered its purchase and installation throughout his offices. Other branches of the Interior Department followed suit. This was a rare occasion when the Patent Office could take immediate advantage of one of the innovative discoveries processed through its system.

Fig. 59
Overcrowding of building, ca. 1901.
This model hall was converted into the Patent Office's public search room, where thousands of files were kept for inspection by patent applicants and other interested parties.

Although the patent staff continued to be overwhelmed by applications, the deluge of patent models finally subsided. The requirement for submitting a model with an application was relaxed in 1870 and discontinued by 1880. New generations of educated and specialized patent examiners could evaluate patents based solely on drawings, specifications, and descriptions. Also, with the development of new electrical, chemical, and other technologies, inventions became more complex and theoretical, obviating the need for a model.

Inevitably the fascination with patent models that had reached its height in the mid-nineteenth century gradually declined. By 1908 most of the patent models were moved into storage, and the vast third-floor exhibition galleries were converted into offices and other uses (see fig. 59). In 1926 the Patent Office disposed of all its models. Given first choice, the Smithsonian acquired 6,000 models, which now reside in the collections of its National Museum of American History. Other models went to other museums and some to the inventors or their families. The majority, however,

Fig. 60
Hansen typewriter, commercial model, ca. 1872. The Remington typewriter was a vast improvement over this earlier invention.

Fig. 61
Remington no. 1 typewriter, commercial model, ca. 1878. The new typewriter was immediately purchased for use throughout the Patent Office.

were sold in bulk at public auction for nominal prices. Most were purchased for a short-lived patent model museum in New York City.

In 1917 the Department of the Interior and its many offices moved from the Patent Office Building to the Interior's newly constructed home in Foggy Bottom, and for the next fifteen years the Patent Office enjoyed the luxury of sole occupancy of its building. Eight years later, the jurisdiction of the Patent Office was transferred to the Commerce Department, which had been created by Congress in 1913. Finally, in 1932 the Patent Office vacated the building it had occupied for ninety-two years and moved into the structure newly built for the Commerce Department near the White House and the Mall. Intended to meet the needs of the Patent Office for fifty years, the building had remarkably done so for almost a century.

That same year the Civil Service Commission took possession of the entire building and remained there for thirty-one years (fig. 62). The noble edifice suffered abuses and "modernization" during these decades. Fluorescent lighting fixtures were installed (fig. 63), and all the skylights of the third floor were covered. Elevators were punched through masonry floors, and ductwork was run through stairways. All the interior stone, woodwork, and walls were painted institutional green, and linoleum was laid over marble floors. Storage became woefully inadequate (fig. 64).

HE IS STILL KEEPING WATCH OVER THE DESTINIES OF THE CIVIL SERVICE COMMISSION

IN MEMORY OF A GREAT PRESIDENT A WARM CIVIL SERVICE ENTHUSIAST AND A VALUED PERSONAL FRIEND

JUNE 1939   Clifford K. Berryman

Fig. 62
Cartoon, 1939. The Patent Office moved out in 1932, and the Civil Service Commission moved into the building. As a member of the Civil Service Commission (1889–95), Theodore Roosevelt had advocated reform.

Fig. 63
Civil Service offices, 1950s. Cubicles and fluorescent lighting were the order of the day.

Fig. 64
Civil Service records, 1935. This basement storage facility left much to be desired.

Fig. 65
Remodeled south entrance. With the widening of F Street in 1936, the steps to the portico were removed, and a new entrance created.

There were other threats to the building as well. Earlier in 1907 and again in 1913, design proposals were advanced to build into the courtyard to alleviate overcrowding; fortunately, they came to naught. In 1925, at the request of local merchants, Congress considered demolishing the building for parking and opening Eighth Street through the middle of the property. The *New York Times* and the American Institute of Architects, among others, objected, and the proposal was dropped. In 1936, to facilitate the flow of traffic, F Street was widened along the south side of the building, necessitating the removal of the great flight of granite steps leading to the second-floor portico. Funded by $100,000 from the Works Progress Administration, local architect Horace W. Peaslee designed a new south entrance at ground level that remains today (fig. 65).

Revival

The greatest threat to the Patent Office Building occurred in 1953 when legislation was introduced in Congress to demolish that noble edifice for a parking garage. The General Services Administration, which had jurisdiction over the building, supported the legislation. Promised a new headquarters in Foggy Bottom, the Civil Service Commission was eager to move out. This time the proposed demolition provoked a furious reaction that rallied many organizations in a three-year effort to save the historic structure. The recently chartered National Trust for Historic Preservation, the Society of Architectural Historians, and the American Institute of Architects joined the fray, calling attention to the building's historic value, architectural significance, good structural condition, enormous space, and government ownership (fig. 66). They cited the irony of retaining the "unsightly temporary war-buildings" intruding on the Mall while planning to demolish the quite usable Patent Office Building.

Influential in these efforts was David E. Finley (fig. 67), director of the National Gallery of Art and chairman of the U.S. Commission of Fine Arts, which was formed in 1910 to approve and protect monuments in Washington. Finley went directly to President Dwight D. Eisenhower in 1955 and persuaded him of the building's historic and architectural importance. Eisenhower immediately ordered both the General Services Administration and the Bureau of the Budget to preserve it. Finley also

Fig. 66
Lincoln Gallery, 1967. The enormous gallery has been cleared of fluorescent lighting, office cubicles, and other excrescences. David Scott, then director of the National Collection of Fine Arts, stands against a column at center.

approached the secretary of the Smithsonian Institution, Leonard Carmichael, about the Smithsonian's use of the structure for a national portrait gallery. In related events, the Smithsonian for many years had pursued efforts to find an appropriate home for its art gallery. Carmichael was delighted at the prospect of acquiring the building for these dual purposes.

At last Congress in 1958 transferred the structure to the Smithsonian "to house certain art collections," leaving the ultimate disposition and naming of the building to the Smithsonian's discretion. As justification for the transfer, Congress noted the Smithsonian's dire need for more exhibition space, the suitability of the architecture for that purpose, and the economy of renovation over new construction. The Civil Service Commission would remain in the building until it could move to new quarters, which it did in 1963.

Saving the structure was a remarkable accomplishment for the time. The importance of historic preservation had not yet penetrated the public conscience. Not until the National Historic Preservation Act was passed in 1966 was official recognition given to preserving the nation's wealth of historic and architectural treasures in cooperation with state and local governments. In 1965 the Patent Office Building was designated a National Historic Landmark—the highest government honor a historic structure can receive—and in 1966 it was listed on the National Register of Historic Places by the Department of the Interior.

To design and supervise the renovation of the Patent Office Building for museum purposes, the Smithsonian in 1962 retained the

Fig. 67
David E. Finley with the Queen Mother, 1954 (detail). Finley was instrumental in saving the Patent Office Building from demolition.

Fig. 68
Renovation in progress, 1965. Workmen have removed later partitions from the second floor of the west wing.

prominent Washington architectural firm of Faulkner, Kingsbury and Stenhouse. Waldron Faulkner was in charge of design, and the General Services Administration managed contracting and construction. Congress appropriated $5,465,000 for the restoration (fig. 68). The Smithsonian's Board of Regents and newly appointed Secretary S. Dillon Ripley decided that the building would house two Smithsonian museums, the recently created National Portrait Gallery and the existing National Collection of Fine Arts (now the Smithsonian American Art Museum). The remodeled structure was named the Fine Arts & Portrait Gallery Building.

The plans drawn by Faulkner for the building's renovation and adaptive museum use were put out to bid by the General Services Administration. When bids exceeded the available appropriation by 35 percent, the scope of the project had to be reduced. A proposed large-scale restaurant and an auditorium were eliminated. The heating, ventilating, and air-conditioning system was scaled down, and where existing marble pavers could not be salvaged, less expensive terrazzo flooring was installed. Work began on December 31, 1964. Despite the modifications, the renovation respected and showcased the building's historic architecture.

Encumbering accretions and expedient alterations were swept away. The interior stonework was cleaned of many layers of green paint, and the building's south sandstone façade was also cleaned, since most of its white paint had worn off due to lack of maintenance. Because so much of the edifice had originally been designed for large open or flexible exhibition galleries, its configuration was compatible with museum use.

The Portrait Gallery was allocated the southern half of the building with its entrance on F Street. The American Art Museum was given the northern half with its entrance on G Street. The two museums' public spaces were connected through the east wing and the open courtyard. Each museum had a sales shop beside its entrance, and a small cafeteria-style restaurant in the east wing served visitors and staff. The spacious courtyard was landscaped much as it appeared in the nineteenth century, with seating areas where visitors could bring food from the restaurant and enjoy the shade of two large elm trees (fig. 69). The only significant exterior modification to the building was the construction under the north portico steps of a loading dock accessed by driveway ramps.

Of the four great galleries on the top floor, the south hall was remodeled for Portrait Gallery offices and display but not fully restored until 1974 (figs. 70, 71, and 72). Because of its length and elaborate Victorian decoration, it was designated the Great Hall. The east hall was returned to Mills's great vaulted room of 1852 and subsequently used by the American Art Museum to showcase its twentieth-century collection. Since it was the only space that remained architecturally intact from Lincoln's inaugural ball, it was named the Lincoln Gallery (fig. 73). The north hall was greatly modified for changing exhibition galleries for American art, and the west room was remodeled into an impressive three-tiered library to serve both museums.

Fig. 69
Courtyard, 1980s. The building's landscaped courtyard—with its large elms, historic cast-iron fountains, and Calder sculptures—was an oasis for diners and visitors.

Fig. 70
Entrance to Model Hall, 1999. This doorway opened from the stairway to the Great Hall.

Fig. 71
Detail of tile floor, 1999. The encaustic tiles imitate the style of the British company Minton, but were manufactured in the United States.

Fig. 72
Great Hall, ca. 1973. The south hall, with its impressive stained-glass dome and colorful decoration, was restored to its original splendor. A medallion portrait of Eli Whitney is set into the wall, at left.

In a Patent Office Building largely restored to its original grandeur, the American Art Museum opened to the public on May 3, 1968. President Lyndon B. Johnson presided over a formal dedication in the courtyard during an evening ceremony (fig. 74). The Portrait Galley opened on October 5, 1968, with bunting, music, and a speech by the mayor of Washington. A reviewer for the *AIA Journal* noted that the challenge was "to take a building that had been virtually vandalized and restore it to health"; he concluded that "while the results in some specific details can be faulted, the achievement, in general, is impressive."

Fig. 73
Lincoln Gallery, ca. 1975. The restored gallery presented a survey of highlights from the American art collection. Its generous spaces later became the venue for twentieth-century American art.

Fig. 74
President Lyndon Johnson at reopening ceremonies, May 3, 1968. The president and the first lady (at right) were guests of honor at the Smithsonian American Art Museum's evening ceremony in the courtyard.

The Museums

The National Portrait Gallery was established by Congress in 1962 as "a free public museum for the exhibition of and study of portraiture and statuary depicting men and women who have made significant contributions to the history, development, and culture of the people of the United States." Modeled on the National Portrait Gallery in London, founded in 1856, the new gallery would undertake a broad approach to the history of the country and the figures who shaped it and not serve merely as a "hall of fame." As the gallery's first director observed, "We have a large task ahead, and as has been said, are starting 100 years too late."

Although the endeavor seemed daunting at first, the Portrait Gallery began to assemble a collection worthy of the nation. Its paintings, sculpture, prints, photographs, and drawings tell myriad stories of American history and character—from colonial times to the present day—and elucidate the art of portraiture. The gallery's collection, which includes one of the largest assemblages of presidential portraits in the country (figs. 75 and 76), is supplemented by an active exhibition program that covers a broad range of topics, including the struggle for independence, self-portraiture, women's suffrage, the Great Depression, musical theater, and science.

Portrait research has been an important component of the National Portrait Gallery since its inception. Its Catalog of American Portraits has amassed documentation for and photographs of approximately 100,000 portraits of historically

Fig. 75
Second floor, south foyer, 1999. The "Lansdowne portrait" of Washington by Gilbert Stuart was featured.

significant Americans or portraits by American artists. The Charles Willson Peale Family Papers, a historical editing project, was established in 1974 and has published six volumes of selected documents.

The Smithsonian American Art Museum has a much longer history than its sister museum. Its genesis was the Smithsonian's accumulation of art over the years, first housed in the Castle and the Arts and Industries Building and in 1910 in a large gallery in what is now the National Museum of Natural History. In the settlement of a bequest in 1906, the Smithsonian's art collection was designated the National Gallery of Art. Substantial collections of European, American, and other art were donated during the next three decades. The Gallery of Art became a separate branch of the Smithsonian in 1920 with its own curator and budget. In 1925 the Smithsonian proposed a grand new building on the Mall for the gallery, but was subsequently stymied by philanthropist Andrew Mellon's plans to donate his unparalleled collection of old-master paintings to the nation. Mellon insisted on the name "National Gallery of Art" for his new museum, so in 1937 Congress obligingly rechristened the Smithsonian's gallery the National Collection of Fine Arts. In a second attempt at a new building, an architectural competition in 1939 was won by the father-and-son team Eliel and

Fig. 76
Hall of Presidents, 1987. The second floor of the south wing, which once housed the Patent Office Library, displayed in chronological order the portraits of the U.S. presidents.

Eero Saarinen. Their striking contemporary building would have been located where the National Air and Space Museum now stands. Unfortunately, funding for the structure never materialized.

The gracious facilities of the refurbished Patent Office Building were a welcome change for the museum, which by its 1968 reopening had focused its acquisitions, exhibitions, and programs exclusively on American art (fig. 77). To establish its identity and mission clearly, the museum in 1980 was officially renamed the National

Fig. 77
Second floor, east corridor, 1978. American art of the nineteenth century was on view.

Museum of American Art. Then, to emphasize its relationship with the Smithsonian, in 2000 it was given its present title, the Smithsonian American Art Museum. The museum holds one of the largest collections of American art in the world, with more than 41,000 objects from colonial times to the present, ranging from fine art to folk art and photography (fig. 78). Over the years, the museum has presented pioneering exhibitions on both individual artists and thematic subjects that proved instrumental in establishing wider appreciation and study of American art (fig. 79).

Research and publication of American art are essential to the museum's mandate. Resources include seven research databases comprising more than 950,000 records, the scholarly journal *American Art,* and an active fellowship program for pre- and post-doctorate study. In 1972 the museum opened the Renwick Gallery, a branch museum that collects and exhibits American craft and decorative arts.

The Archives of American Art joined the Smithsonian in 1970 and established offices in the library of the Patent Office Building. Organized in 1954, the Archives recognized that invaluable papers of American artists were being lost or dispersed at an alarming rate. Letters, diaries, sketchbooks, photographs, journals, and other documents were collected from artists, dealers, collectors, and historians over the years, microfilmed, and then made available to researchers in several field offices strategically located around the country. The collection, now expanded to include

Fig. 78
Second floor, north wing, 1982. Visitors admire a painting by Albert Bierstadt.

Fig. 79
Granite Gallery, 1981. The gallery on the first floor of the west wing was named for its large granite piers. The terrazzo floor is from the 1960s renovation.

oral histories, encompasses over fourteen million items and is the largest primary source of documentation on American art in the world.

As the staffs, collections, and programs for the museums doubled and trebled over the years, space increasingly became a problem. The Smithsonian attempted to acquire the historic General Post Office Building across the street, which was designed by Robert Mills and completed by Thomas U. Walter, but funding for its renovation was not forthcoming. The deteriorating physical condition of the Patent Office Building reached a crisis in 1997 when pipes under pressure began bursting in the attic, sending floods of water to the galleries below, sometimes in the middle of the night. The heating-ventilating-air-conditioning system that was inadequate when first installed had outlived its useful life, and a completely new climate control system with ductwork was now mandatory.

Other compromises made in the 1960s renovation as a result of budget constraints required rectifying. An auditorium was at the top of the list of sorely needed facilities. The building also lacked up-to-date wiring and technological infrastructure for electronic communication. By 1999 the Smithsonian decided that a complete top-to-bottom renovation and modernization of the Patent Office Building was essential. The award-winning local firm of Hartman-Cox Architects was selected to design and oversee the work, with Warren Cox and Mary Kay Lanzillotta as the lead architects.

Renovation

Renovation of the Patent Office Building began in 1998 with the restoring and reopening of the large skylights in the east, south, and west wings. For the first time in decades, natural light—filtered against ultraviolet damage—poured into the top-floor halls. At the same time, a new two-acre copper roof was installed, duplicating the original nineteenth-century design and materials as closely as possible (fig. 80). In 2000 the building was closed to the public, and all staff, collections, library, and support facilities were moved to other locations, where most will remain after the building reopens to make way for improved visitor amenities and expanded gallery display. Then the work began to convert the vacated spaces to new uses while maintaining the historic structure's architectural integrity (fig. 81).

A dramatic change in the building came with the decision to excavate the open courtyard for an underground auditorium, the only possible location for such a large unobstructed space. The museums' diverse offering of educational and scholarly programs will now take advantage of the new 346-seat Nan Tucker McEvoy Auditorium (fig. 82). With its state-of-the-art facilities, the auditorium can accommodate theatrical and musical performances as well as multimedia presentations.

Removal of the elm trees from the courtyard—necessitated after they contracted Dutch elm disease—provided an opportunity to enclose that open

Fig. 80
Installation of copper roof, 1998. The new roof replicated the original as closely as possible.

space with a glass canopy so the courtyard could be used year-round for dining, installations, and large-scale events. Renowned architect Norman Foster of Foster and Partners in London was chosen to design a self-supporting contemporary canopy that will float over the courtyard as a reflection of the changing needs of today's museums. The enclosed 28,000-square-foot courtyard, named in honor of donors Robert and Arlene Kogod, will be one of the largest unobstructed historic interior spaces in the nation's capital (fig. 83). Construction of the canopy is scheduled to be completed in 2007.

Other features have been incorporated into the old building. The third-floor library in the west wing has been refitted as the Luce Foundation Center for American Art, housing in glass cases more than 3,500 artworks from the Smithsonian American Art Museum's collection. Visitors can now peruse in "visible storage" a vast array of material that cannot be accommodated in the public galleries (fig. 84). A first of its kind in any museum is the Lunder Conservation Center, adjacent to the visible storage. There, the activities of the museums' conservators, in what were previously behind-the-scenes laboratories, are fully exposed through floor-to-ceiling glass walls so that visitors may observe them as they treat paintings,

Fig. 81
Renovation of second floor, north wing, 2003. With the ceiling removed, the segmental brick arches supported on iron I-beams are visible.

Fig. 82
McEvoy Auditorium, digital concept.

Fig. 83
Kogod Courtyard with glass canopy, digital concept.

drawings, photographs, and other objects with the latest equipment (fig. 85). Live-camera displays, an interactive media wall, and interpretive kiosks will explain the conservation process.

The remodeling of the Patent Office Building brought a sea change to the spatial functioning of the National Portrait Gallery and the Smithsonian American Art Museum. Rather than separate entrances for each museum, they now share both entrances, with the principal entrance on the south, and the north entrance to serve tour groups and provide access to a greatly expanded

Fig. 84
Luce Foundation Center for American Art, artist's concept. More than 3,500 American artworks are on view in this visible storage facility.

museum shop and restaurant on the first floor of the north wing. Galleries for each museum's collections and changing exhibitions have also been relocated.

Complete new electrical, communications, security, plumbing, and lighting systems have been installed, often in new conduits under the floors. The floors in all hallways and in the Lincoln Gallery are now paved in marble patterns matching the nineteenth-century originals as closely as possible. The magnificent encaustic tile floor in the south wing's Great Hall, which had badly deteriorated, was replicated exactly in England and replaced. More than 550 windows were replaced, including handblown glass ordered from Poland to simulate the slight irregularities of old panes.

State-of-the-art heating and air-conditioning systems were installed to maintain modern museum standards for climate control. The challenge was to design the systems' massive ductwork and mechanical support without destroying the historic architecture of a building constructed of masonry walls on two city blocks around a courtyard. Although the location of old chimney flues was known, sonar was used to detect undiscovered chases in the walls for the new ductwork. Other surprises discovered during the course of the work included an abandoned well in the courtyard that had been covered over and graffiti on woodwork in the

Fig. 85
Lunder Conservation Center, artist's concept. Visitors can watch conservators at work and access computer kiosks explaining the conservation process.

Lincoln Gallery, dated 1864 by an unidentified "C. H. F.," now preserved for inspection by visitors.

In October 2005, the Donald W. Reynolds Foundation made a $45-million gift to the Smithsonian to help complete the building's renovation and enhancements. In recognition of this gift, the two museums and all the attendant public amenities, including the courtyard, are collectively known as the Donald W. Reynolds Center for American Art and Portraiture. After more than six years of renovation, this "noblest of Washington buildings" reopened in July 2006. The cost of the renovation and enhancements included more than $100 million privately raised and $166 million appropriated by Congress.

For almost two hundred years, the Patent Office Building has witnessed a parade of history and experienced many changes of fortune (fig. 86). One scholar has summarized its enduring significance: "The Patent Office Building, more than any other American building of its time, reflected the achievements and ambitions of the American nation. Its classical stone façade was a simple and powerful statement of the expected durability of American institutions, just as its austere and utilitarian interior design spoke of republican practicality and taste. Its exhibitions celebrated the discoveries and resources of the nation and the creative potential of every citizen." With its recent renovation for the two museums, the building will even better serve the country's creative genius. The 1836 Congressional report authorizing construction of the building called for "a place to celebrate and present the achievement of the American people." As it begins its third century of useful life, the venerable Patent Office Building perpetuates this transcendent purpose.

Fig. 86
Evening view, ca. 1978. The Patent Office Building remains one of the great landmarks of the nation's capital.

Notes

page 9: "a temple of invention." The phrase has been used in variations over the years. See Douglas E. Evelyn, "Exhibiting America: The Patent Office as Cultural Artifact," *Smithsonian Studies in American Art* (Summer 1989): 35.

page 13: "onerous to the courts, ruinous to the parties..." Rafael A. Crespo, "The History of the Patent Office Building," unpublished MS, 1988, p. 12. Office of Architectural History and Historic Preservation, Smithsonian Institution.

page 15: "It is sometimes called the City of Magnificent Distances..." Charles Dickens, *American Notes for General Circulation* (London: Chapman and Hall, 1863), p. 5. Originally published 1855.

page 15: "I was delighted with the whole aspect of Washington...." Frances Trollope, *Domestic Manners of the Americans with a History of Mrs. Trollope's Adventures in America*, ed. Donald Smalley (New York: Alfred A. Knopf, 1949), p. 216. Originally published 1832.

page 18: "The patent system added..." Abraham Lincoln, "Lincoln's Second Lecture on Discoveries and Inventions, delivered February 11, 1859, in Jacksonville, Ill.," in *Collected Works of Abraham Lincoln*, vol. 3, ed. Roy P. Basler (New Brunswick, NJ: Rutgers University Press, 1955), p. 363.

page 23: "I have always deprecated..." John M. Bryan, "Robert Mills: Education and Early Drawings," in *Robert Mills, Architect*, ed. John M. Bryan (Washington, D.C.: American Institute of Architects, 1989), p. 2, see note 5.

page 24: "Robert Mills as Architect to aid in forming the plans..." Andrew Jackson as quoted in Robert W. Fenwick, "Old and New Patent Office," *Proceedings and Addresses, Celebration of the Beginning of the Second Century of the American Patent System at Washington City, D.C., April 8, 9, 10, 1891* (Washington, D.C.: Gedney & Roberts Co., 1892), p. 461.

page 25: "had come well-recommended." William P. Elliot as quoted in "Notes from W. P. Elliot's Diary" (July 7, 1836), in Robert W. Fenwick, "Old and New Patent Office," *Proceedings and Addresses, Celebration of the Beginning of the Second Century of the American Patent System at Washington City, D.C., April 8, 9, 10, 1891* (Washington, D.C.: Gedney & Roberts Co., 1892), p. 464.

page 26: "resorted to every means to injure my professional standing." Douglas E. Evelyn, "The Washington Years: The U.S. Patent Office," in *Robert Mills, Architect*, ed. John M. Bryan (Washington, D.C.: American Institute of Architects, 1989), see note 32.

page 27: "Poor patentees! Not a model..." Rafael A. Crespo, "The History of the Patent Office Building," unpublished MS, 1988, p. 22. Office of Architectural History and Historic Preservation, Smithsonian Institution.

page 27: "appreciation of Mr. Elliot's talents..." Douglas E. Evelyn, "The Washington Years: The U.S. Patent Office," in *Robert Mills, Architect*, ed. John M. Bryan (Washington, D.C.: American Institute of Architects, 1989), see note 32.

page 34: "I cannot consent that my mortal body..." March 27, 1845, letter from Andrew Jackson to the Hon. J. D. Elliott, in *A Popular Catalogue of the Extraordinary Curiosities in the National Institute, Arranged in the Building Belonging to the Patent Office* (Washington, D.C.: Alfred Hunter, 1859), p. 39.

page 46: "Any blow... I have got above them." Elizabeth Brown Pryor, *Clara Barton, Professional Angel* (Philadelphia: University of Pennsylvania Press, 1987), p. 61, see note 34.

page 51: "A few weeks ago the vast area..." Walt Whitman, *Specimen Days, February 23*, in *Walt Whitman Complete Poetry and Collected Prose*, (New York: Literary Classics of the United States, 1982), p. 717.

page 53: "I have been up to look at the dance..." Walt Whitman, *Specimen Days, March 6*, in *Walt Whitman Complete Poetry and Collected Prose* (New York: Literary Classics of the United States, 1982), p. 761.

page 54: "trying to throw off care for a while," and page 57, "In less than an hour the table..." *New-York Times*, "The Inauguration Ball," March 8, 1865.

page 57: "The floor of the supper room..." *Washington Evening Star*, 2nd edition, 25, no. 3749, "The Inauguration Ball," March 8, 1865.

page 74: "Cluss is one of our best and most talented people." Karl Marx to Josef Weydemeyer, December 19, 1851, in *Marx-Engel's Gesamtausgabe* III/4 (Berlin: Dietz Verlag, 1987), pp. 276–77.

page 93: "to take a building that had been..." Wilcomb E. Washburn, "Temple of the Arts: The Renovation of Washington's Patent Office Building," *AIA Journal* (March 1969; repr.): 61.

page 95: "We have a large task ahead..." Margaret Christman, "The National Portrait Gallery," in *A Brush with History: Paintings from the National Portrait Gallery*, eds. Carolyn Kinder Carr and Ellen G. Miles (Washington, D.C.: National Portrait Gallery, Smithsonian Institution, 2001).

page 106: "The Patent Office Building, more than any other..." Douglas E. Evelyn, "Exhibiting America: The Patent Office as Cultural Artifact," *Smithsonian Studies in American Art* (Summer 1989): 35.

Selected Bibliography

"An Account of the Destruction by Fire of the North and West Halls of the Model Room in the United States Patent Office Building on the 24th of September 1877." Washington, D.C., October 23, 1877.

Bryan, John M., ed. *Robert Mills, Architect*. Essays by Robert L. Alexander, John M. Bryan, Douglas E. Evelyn, and Pamela Scott. Washington, D.C.: American Institute of Architects, 1989.

Davies, Jane B. "A. J. Davis' Projects for a Patent Office Building, 1832–1834." *Journal of the Society of Architectural Historians* 24 no. 3 (October 1965; repr.): 229–51.

———. "Six Letters by William P. Elliot to Alexander Jackson Davis, 1834–1838." *Journal of the Society of Architectural Historians* 26 (March 1967): 71–73.

Del Donna, Elizabeth B. "The Museum Collections of the Patent Office Building, 1841–1881." Smithsonian American Art Museum/National Portrait Gallery Library. Unpublished MS, 1965.

———. "Patent Office Building Competition, Washington, D.C., 1878." *Journal of the Society of Architectural Historians* 23 (March 1964): 44–48.

———. "Reconstruction of the Patent Office Building, 1878–1886." Smithsonian American Art Museum/National Portrait Gallery Library. Unpublished MS, 1965.

Dobyns, Kenneth W. *The Patent Office Pony: A History of the Early Patent Office*. Fredericksburg, VA: Sergeant Kirkland's Museum and Historical Society, 1997.

Evans, George W. "The Birth and Growth of the Patent Office." *Records of the Columbia Historical Society of Washington, D.C.* (1919): 105–124.

Evelyn, Douglas E. "Exhibiting America: The Patent Office as Cultural Artifact." *Smithsonian Studies in American Art* (Summer 1989): 25–37.

———. "The National Gallery at the Patent Office." *Magnificent Voyagers: The U.S. Exploring Expedition, 1838–1842*. Herman J. Viola and Carolyn Margolis, eds., with assistance of Jan S. Davis and Sharon D. Galperin. Washington, D.C.: Smithsonian Institution Press, (1985): 227–41.

———. *A Public Building for a New Democracy: The Patent Office Building in the Nineteenth Century*. PhD diss. George Washington University, 1997.

Fenwick, Robert W. "Old and New Patent Office," *Proceedings and Addresses, Celebration of the Beginning of the Second Century of the American Patent System at Washington City, D.C., April 8, 9, 10, 1891* (Washington, D.C.: Gedney & Roberts Co., 1892): 453–71.

Green, Constance McLaughlin. *Washington, Village and Capital, 1800–1878*. Princeton, NJ: Princeton University Press, 1962.

Grissom, C. A., Charola, A. E., and Henriques, F. M. A. "To Paint Or Not to Paint. A Difficult Decision." *Protection and Conservation of the Cultural Heritage of the Mediterranean Cities*. Emilio Galán and Fulvio Zezza, eds. Lisse, Netherlands: Swets and Zeitlinger, 2002.

Hunter, Alfred. *A Popular Catalogue of the Extraordinary Curiosities in the National Institute, Arranged in the Building Belonging to the Patent Office*. Washington, D.C.: Alfred Hunter, 1859.

Janssen, Barbara Suit. *Icons of Invention: American Patent Models*. Washington, D.C.: National Museum of American History, Smithsonian Institution, 1990.

Leech, Margaret. *Reveille in Washington: 1860–1865*. New York: Carroll & Graf Publishers, 1986.

Lessoff, Alan and Christof Mauch, eds. *Adolf Cluss, Architect: From Germany to America*. New York: The Historical Society of Washington, D.C., and Stadtarchiv Heilbronn in association with Berghahn Books, 2005.

Melder, Keith E. *City of Magnificent Intentions: A History of Washington, District of Columbia*, 2nd ed. Washington, D.C.: Intac, 1997.

Morris, Roy, Jr. *The Better Angel: Walt Whitman in the Civil War*. Oxford: Oxford University Press, 2000.

New-York Times. "The Inauguration Ball." March 8, 1865.

The Patent Office Building Historic Structures Report, vols. 1 and 2. Prepared for Office of Physical Plant, Smithsonian Institution, Washington, D.C., Hartman-Cox Architects, Oehrlein and Associates Architects, April 6, 1999.

Pryor, Elizabeth Brown. *Clara Barton, Professional Angel*. Philadelphia: University of Pennsylvania Press, 1987.

Reps, John W. *Monumental Washington: The Planning and Development of the Capital Center*. Princeton, NJ: Princeton University Press, 1967.

United States Magazine 3 no. 4, "The City of Washington." (October 1856): 289–98; and no. 5 (November 1856): 433–43.

Washburn, Wilcomb E. "Temple of the Arts: The Renovation of Washington's Patent Office Building." *AIA Journal* (March 1969; repr.): 54–61.

Washington Evening Star 25, no. 3749, 2nd ed. "The Inauguration Ball." March 8, 1865.

Wojcik, Susan Brizzolara. "Thomas Ustick Walter." *American National Biography*, vol. 22. John A. Garraty and Mark C. Carnes, eds. American Council of Learned Societies. Oxford: Oxford University Press (1999): 583–85.

Illustration Sources and Credits

Beginnings. Fig. 1, National Museum of American History, Smithsonian Institution (catalogue no. T. 8756); Fig. 2, Engraving by Charles Balthazar Julian Févret de Saint-Mémin; National Portrait Gallery, Smithsonian Institution, gift of Mr. and Mrs. Paul Mellon; Fig. 3, Watercolor attributed to Nicholas King; Huntington Library, Art Collections and Botanical Gardens; Fig. 4, United States Patent and Trademark Office.

The Turning Point. Fig. 5, Painting by George Cooke; White House Collection (545), courtesy of the White House Historical Association; Fig. 6, Painting by Albert Gallatin Hoit; courtesy of Maine State Museum, Augusta, Maine; Fig. 7, Photograph courtesy of Tippecanoe County Historical Association, Lafayette, Indiana; Fig. 8, Painting by Ralph E. W. Earl; Smithsonian American Art Museum, transfer from U.S. District Court for the District of Columbia; Fig. 9, All rights reserved, Metropolitan Museum of Art, Harris Brisbane Dick Fund, 1924; Fig. 10, James H. Dakin Collection, Louisiana Division, New Orleans Public Library.

Robert Mills in Charge. Fig. 11, Daguerreotype by Jesse H. Whitehurst; National Portrait Gallery, Smithsonian Institution, gift of Richard Evans; Fig. 12, Atlas by Henry S. Tanner; Historical Society of Washington, D.C.; Fig. 13, Daguerreotype by John Plumbe Jr.; Library of Congress; Fig. 14, Illustration from *United States Magazine* 3, no. 5 (November 1856); National Portrait Gallery, Smithsonian Institution; Fig. 15, Lithograph by P. Haas, Washington, D.C.; Library of Congress.

A Museum of Curiosities. Fig. 16, Illustration from the *U.S. Democratic Review,* 1856; National Portrait Gallery, Smithsonian Institution; Fig. 17, Pamphlet published by Alfred Hunter, Washington, D.C., 1855; Library of Congress; Figs. 18

and 19, Illustrations from *United States Magazine* 3 no. 4 (October 1856); National Portrait Gallery, Smithsonian Institution; Fig. 20, National Museum of American History, Smithsonian Institution; Fig. 21, National Museum of American History, Smithsonian Institution (patent no. 6489); Fig. 22, National Portrait Gallery, Smithsonian Institution.

Era of Expansion. Fig. 23, Chromolithograph by Edward Sachse & Co.; National Portrait Gallery, Smithsonian Institution; Fig. 24, Smithsonian American Art Museum; Fig. 25, Glass-plate image by Frederick Langenheim; National Museum of American History, Smithsonian Institution, Photographic History Collection, Behring Center; Fig. 26, Daguerreotype; National Portrait Gallery, Smithsonian Institution; Fig. 27, Illustration from *United States Magazine* 3, no. 5 (November 1856); National Portrait Gallery, Smithsonian Institution; Fig. 28, National Portrait Gallery, Smithsonian Institution; Fig. 29, Photograph by Mathew Brady Studio; National Archives and Records Administration.

The Civil War Years. Fig. 30, Hand-colored illustration from *Harper's Weekly,* June 1, 1861; National Portrait Gallery, Smithsonian Institution; Fig. 31, National Portrait Gallery, Smithsonian Institution; Fig. 32, Photograph by Mathew Brady; National Portrait Gallery, Smithsonian Institution, gift of Mr. and Mrs. Charles Feinberg; Fig. 33, Whitman notebook, 1862, pg. 3, Library of Congress, Manuscript Division, Thomas Biggs Harned Walt Whitman Collection.

Lincoln's Inaugural Ball. Fig. 34, Courtesy of the Clara Barton National Historic Site, National Park Service, U.S. Department of the Interior; Fig. 35, Photograph by Mathew Brady; National Portrait Gallery, Smithsonian Institution; Fig. 36, Photograph by the Mathew Brady Studio; National Portrait Gallery,

Smithsonian Institution, Meserve Collection; Fig 37, Illustration from *Illustrated London News,* April 8, 1865; National Portrait Gallery, Smithsonian Institution; Fig. 38, Library of Congress.

Completion of the Building. Fig. 39, Lithograph by John Bachmann; Historical Society of Washington, D.C.; Fig. 40, Stereoview by Kilburn Brothers, Littleton, New Hampshire; National Portrait Gallery, Smithsonian Institution; Fig. 41, Stereoview by Bell and Brothers; National Portrait Gallery, Smithsonian Institution; Fig. 42, Lithograph by Edmund Masson; National Portrait Gallery, Smithsonian Institution; Fig. 43, National Museum of American History, Smithsonian Institution (patent no. 6420); Fig. 44, National Museum of American History, Smithsonian Institution (patent no. 174465); Fig. 45, National Museum of American History, Smithsonian Institution (patent no. 19405); Fig. 46, National Museum of American History, Smithsonian Institution (patent no. 19015); Fig. 47, Smithsonian American Art Museum; Fig. 48, Smithsonian American Art Museum/National Portrait Gallery Library, Smithsonian Institution; Fig. 49, Library of Congress.

The Conflagration. Figs. 50, 51, 52, and 53, Illustrations from *Daily Graphic,* New York, September 28, 1877; National Portrait Gallery, Smithsonian Institution; Fig. 54, Photolithograph by Norris Peters, Washington, D.C.; National Archives and Records Administration.

Rebuilding. Fig. 55, Photolithograph by Norris Peters from drawing by Cluss & Schulze Architects: National Portrait Gallery, Smithsonian Institution, gift of Norman Evans; Fig. 56, Photograph by National Archives and Records Administration; Fig. 57, Photograph by Peter Fink, 1967, for National Museum of American Art, Smithsonian Institution; Fig. 58, Photolithograph of drawing by

Cluss & Schulze Architects; Office of Architectural History and Historic Preservation, Smithsonian Institution.

Decline. Fig. 59, National Portrait Gallery, Smithsonian Institution; Fig. 60, National Museum of American History, Smithsonian Institution (catalogue no. 181005); Fig. 61, National Museum of American History, Smithsonian Institution (catalogue no. 181132); Fig. 62, Cartoon by Clifford K. Berryman; National Archives and Records Administration, Records of the Office of Personnel Management; Fig. 63, Smithsonian American Art Museum; Fig. 64, National Archives and Records Administration; Fig. 65, Smithsonian American Art Museum/National Portrait Gallery Library, Smithsonian Institution.

Revival. Fig. 66, Office of Facilities Engineering and Operations, Smithsonian Institution; Fig. 67, National Gallery of Art, Washington, D.C., Gallery Archives; Fig. 68, Photograph by Grunley-Walsh Construction Co.; Office of Architectural History and Historic Preservation, Smithsonian Institution; Figs. 69, 70, 71, and 72, National Portrait Gallery, Smithsonian Institution; Figs. 73 and 74, Smithsonian American Art Museum.

The Museums. Figs. 75 and 76, National Portrait Gallery, Smithsonian Institution; Figs. 77, 78, and 79, Smithsonian American Art Museum.

Renovation. Figs. 80 and 81, Office of Facilities Engineering and Operations, Smithsonian Institution; Fig. 82, Image by Interface Multimedia; Smithsonian American Art Museum; Fig. 83, Norman Foster and Partners; Figs. 84 and 85, Images by Academy Studios, Smithsonian American Art Museum; and Fig. 86, National Portrait Gallery, Smithsonian Institution.

Index

This book was typeset in Monotype Baskerville. The original
typeface was designed by Englishman John Baskerville and
appeared in a series of books from 1754 to 1775, including
his masterpiece, a Bible printed for the University of
Cambridge. The font epitomized neoclassicism in type and
closely corresponded to the Greek Revival style in American
architecture, exemplified by the Patent Office Building.